America’s Prisons

Other Books of Related Interest:

Opposing Viewpoints Series

Crime and Criminals

Criminal Justice

Domestic Violence

Mandatory Minimum Sentencing

Current Controversies Series

Family Violence

Guns and Violence

Torture

At Issue Series

Guns and Crime

Homeland Security

Mental Illness and Criminal Behavior

Violent Children

“Congress shall make no law . . . abridging the freedom of speech, or of the press.”

First Amendment to the U.S. Constitution

The basic foundation of our democracy is the First Amendment guarantee of freedom of expression. The Opposing Viewpoints Series is dedicated to the concept of this basic freedom and the idea that it is more important to practice it than to enshrine it.

America's Prisons

Noah Berlatsky, Book Editor

GREENHAVEN PRESS
A part of Gale, Cengage Learning

Detroit • New York • San Francisco • New Haven, Conn • Waterville, Maine • London

Christine Nasso, *Publisher*
Elizabeth Des Chenes, *Managing Editor*

For more information, contact:
Greenhaven Press
27500 Drake Rd.
Farmington Hills, MI 48331-3535
Or you can visit our Internet site at gale.cengage.com

Articles in Greenhaven Press anthologies are often edited for length to meet page requirements. In addition, original titles of these works are changed to clearly present the main thesis and to explicitly indicate the author's opinion. Every effort is made to ensure that Greenhaven Press accurately reflects the original intent of the authors. Every effort has been made to trace the owners of copyrighted material.

LIBRARY OF CONGRESS CATALOGING-IN-PUBLICATION DATA

America's prisons / Noah Berlatsky, book editor.
p. cm. -- (Opposing viewpoints)
Includes bibliographical references and index.
ISBN 978-0-7377-4956-4 (hardcover) -- ISBN 978-0-7377-4957-1 (pbk.)
1. Prisons--United States--Juvenile literature. 2. Imprisonment--United States--Juvenile literature. 3. Alternatives to imprisonment--United States--Juvenile literature. 4. Criminals--Rehabilitation--United States--Juvenile literature. I. Berlatsky, Noah.
HV9471.A487 2010
365'.973--dc22

2009050927

Printed in the United States of America
1 2 3 4 5 6 7 14 13 12 11 10

Contents

Why Consider Opposing Viewpoints? 11

Introduction 14

Chapter 1: Are American Prisons Effective?

Chapter Preface 18

1. Prison Deters Crime 20
Bruce Bayley

2. Prison Does Not Deter Crime 25
Joel Waldfogel

3. Prisons Can Rehabilitate 30
Shreveport Times

4. Prison Rehabilitation Efforts Are Ineffective 35
Dana Pico

5. Alternative Sentencing Would Be More Effective Than Prison 40
Ruth David

6. Alternatives to Prison Are Dangerous and Ineffective 48
Thomas Sowell

Periodical Bibliography 53

Chapter 2: Are American Prisons Just?

Chapter Preface 55

1. America's Imprisonment Practices Are Racist 57
Glenn Loury

2. America's Imprisonment Practices Are Not Racist 71
Heather Mac Donald

3. Mandatory Minimum Sentencing Is Just in Drug Cases **86**
Jodi L. Avergun

4. Mandatory Minimum Sentencing Is Unjust **92**
Robert Hooker and Robert Hirsh

5. Imprisoning Drug Users Is Just **98**
Theodore Dalrymple

6. Imprisoning Nonviolent Drug Users Is Unjust **104**
Michael Huemer

7. Disenfranchising Prisoners Is Just **112**
Ben Johnson

8. Disenfranchising Prisoners Is Unjust **117**
Conor Clarke and Greg Yothers

Periodical Bibliography **121**

Chapter 3: Are American Prisons Humane?

Chapter Preface **123**

1. American Prisons Are Humane **125**
Harley G. Lappin

2. Overcrowding in American Prisons Is Inhumane **131**
Craig Haney

3. Stun Technology Makes Prisons Safer **139**
Jeff Wiehe

4. Stun Technology Is Inhumane and Dangerous **145**
Anne-Marie Cusac

5. California Must Spend More on Prison Health Care **151**
J. Clark Kelso

6. California Should Not Spend Excessively on Prison Health Care *Debra Saunders* 156

Periodical Bibliography 161

Chapter 4: How Should Different Prison Populations Be Treated?

Chapter Preface 163

1. Allowing Inmate Moms to Raise Their Children in Prison Is Beneficial *Suzanne Smalley* 165

2. Raising Children in Prison May Be Harmful *Carol Lloyd* 170

3. Juveniles Should Not Be Placed in Adult Prisons *Campaign for Youth Justice* 174

4. Life Without Parole in the Adult System Is Reasonable for Some Juvenile Offenders *Charles D. Stimson and Andrew M. Grossman* 180

5. The Mentally Ill Should Not Be Placed in the Prison System *Jamie Fellner* 186

6. Focusing on Mental Illness in Prison Prevents Real Reform *Susan Mortimer* 193

Periodical Bibliography 199

For Further Discussion 200

Organizations to Contact 202

Bibliography of Books 208

Index 212

Why Consider Opposing Viewpoints?

> *"The only way in which a human being can make some approach to knowing the whole of a subject is by hearing what can be said about it by persons of every variety of opinion and studying all modes in which it can be looked at by every character of mind. No wise man ever acquired his wisdom in any mode but this."*
>
> *John Stuart Mill*

In our media-intensive culture it is not difficult to find differing opinions. Thousands of newspapers and magazines and dozens of radio and television talk shows resound with differing points of view. The difficulty lies in deciding which opinion to agree with and which "experts" seem the most credible. The more inundated we become with differing opinions and claims, the more essential it is to hone critical reading and thinking skills to evaluate these ideas. Opposing Viewpoints books address this problem directly by presenting stimulating debates that can be used to enhance and teach these skills. The varied opinions contained in each book examine many different aspects of a single issue. While examining these conveniently edited opposing views, readers can develop critical thinking skills such as the ability to compare and contrast authors' credibility, facts, argumentation styles, use of persuasive techniques, and other stylistic tools. In short, the Opposing Viewpoints Series is an ideal way to attain the higher-level thinking and reading skills so essential in a culture of diverse and contradictory opinions.

In addition to providing a tool for critical thinking, Opposing Viewpoints books challenge readers to question their own strongly held opinions and assumptions. Most people form their opinions on the basis of upbringing, peer pressure, and personal, cultural, or professional bias. By reading carefully balanced opposing views, readers must directly confront new ideas as well as the opinions of those with whom they disagree. This is not to argue simplistically that everyone who reads opposing views will—or should—change his or her opinion. Instead, the series enhances readers' understanding of their own views by encouraging confrontation with opposing ideas. Careful examination of others' views can lead to the readers' understanding of the logical inconsistencies in their own opinions, perspective on why they hold an opinion, and the consideration of the possibility that their opinion requires further evaluation.

Evaluating Other Opinions

To ensure that this type of examination occurs, Opposing Viewpoints books present all types of opinions. Prominent spokespeople on different sides of each issue as well as well-known professionals from many disciplines challenge the reader. An additional goal of the series is to provide a forum for other, less known, or even unpopular viewpoints. The opinion of an ordinary person who has had to make the decision to cut off life support from a terminally ill relative, for example, may be just as valuable and provide just as much insight as a medical ethicist's professional opinion. The editors have two additional purposes in including these less known views. One, the editors encourage readers to respect others' opinions—even when not enhanced by professional credibility. It is only by reading or listening to and objectively evaluating others' ideas that one can determine whether they are worthy of consideration. Two, the inclusion of such viewpoints encourages the important critical thinking skill of objectively evaluating an author's credentials and bias. This evaluation will illuminate an author's reasons for taking a particular stance on an issue and will aid in readers' evaluation of the author's ideas.

It is our hope that these books will give readers a deeper understanding of the issues debated and an appreciation of the complexity of even seemingly simple issues when good and honest people disagree. This awareness is particularly important in a democratic society such as ours in which people enter into public debate to determine the common good. Those with whom one disagrees should not be regarded as enemies but rather as people whose views deserve careful examination and may shed light on one's own.

Thomas Jefferson once said that "difference of opinion leads to inquiry, and inquiry to truth." Jefferson, a broadly educated man, argued that "if a nation expects to be ignorant and free . . . it expects what never was and never will be." As individuals and as a nation, it is imperative that we consider the opinions of others and examine them with skill and discernment. The Opposing Viewpoints Series is intended to help readers achieve this goal.

David L. Bender and Bruno Leone,
Founders

Introduction

> *"There is one aspect of society . . . that has continued to expand despite the difficult economic circumstances: the prison population."*
>
> —*Carneades, "Private Prisons: A Reliable American Growth Industry,"* Seeking Alpha, *August 21, 2009. http://seekingalpha.com.*

Prisons are expensive. One of the ways that states have tried to cut costs is by contracting with private companies to run the prisons on behalf of the government.

Private prisons have become an especially popular option following the economic downturn that began in 2008, a situation that led to budget crises in many states. In a November 19, 2008, article in the *Wall Street Journal*, Stephanie Chen reports that private prisons can reduce costs to the state by as much as 15 percent, in part because they have lower payrolls. Chen also notes that the biggest private prison operator in the country, Corrections Corporation of America (CCA) was expanding existing facilities and building more prisons in anticipation of increased demand. Chen quotes CCA's president as stating, "'There is going to be a larger opportunity for us in the future.'"

The libertarian Reason Foundation has been at the forefront of arguing that private prisons benefit the state, the taxpayer, and the prisoners themselves. In a November 1, 2002, article on the foundation's Web site, Geoffrey Segal argues that "six reputable independent studies found quality in the private prisons to be at least as high as in government prisons." Segal maintains, in addition, that private prison operators are bound by contracts that explicitly set forth prisoner rights, whereas government prisons rely on less-clear legal precedents. Further, he points out that "private prisons are monitored by state inspectors" whereas "government correctional departments police themselves, with obvious conflict of interest." Leonard Gilroy, another author on the Reason Foundation Web site, writes in a January 16, 2009, article that states can save up to $15 million a year by outsourcing prisons to private companies, a fact that given the "recession and economic crisis is more important now than ever."

Louise Grant, a spokesperson for CCA, adds that private prisons can be part of the solution to one of the major problems facing prisons in the United States: overcrowding. In a letter to the editor of the *Colorado Springs Gazette* on September 22, 2009, Grant points out that overcrowded prisons are dangerous for inmates and staff, and prevent rehabilitation. The use of private prisons, Grant observes, could "relieve overcrowding," ensuring that "the entire state correctional system is safer."

Critics of private prisons, on the other hand, argue that businesses cut corners on prison staffing, making the prisons less safe and less humane. In a March 7, 2007, article in *Rocky Mountain News*, for example, Alan Gathright notes that following a 2004 riot at a prison in Crowley County, Colorado, "a state auditor blasted CCA for having a staff-to-inmate ratio that was one-seventh of a state prison." Gathright also reports that guards in CCA prisons are paid an average of $24,000, while regular state prison guards are paid an average of $31,000. Critics worry that the low salaries will attract less-qualified workers or make retention of quality staff difficult. Thus, for example, in 2009 the Texas Senate Criminal Justice Committee issued an interim report in which they note that for 2008, "correctional officer turnover rate at the seven private prisons was 90 percent," much higher than the 24 percent turnover rate in state-run prisons. A 90 percent turnover rate means that 90 percent of personnel leave the job within the year, a rate that many observers agree could seriously affect the functioning of the prison.

Critics have also charged that, despite government oversight, abuses at private prisons are often ignored. In a July 30, 2007, article in the *Dallas Morning News*, Holly Becka and Jennifer LaFleur quote Michele Deitch, a prison privatization researcher, as stating, "'Private facilities tend to have many more problems in performance, such as higher levels of assaults, escapes, idleness.'" Becka and LaFleur report also that private companies running juvenile detention centers in Texas have multiple problems, including "inadequate care for inmates." They charge that abuses at the facilities were responsible for the suicide of at least one juvenile, Robert Schulze, who hanged himself at the Coke County Juvenile Justice Center. Becka and LaFleur also note that the Texas Youth Commission in charge of overseeing private juvenile prisons only "rarely" fires contractors for poor performance.

Private prisons ultimately raise many of the same questions for society as do state-run prisons. Some of the most important of these questions are reflected in the chapter titles of *Opposing Viewpoints: America's Prisons:* Are American Prisons Effective? Are American Prisons Just? Are American Prisons Humane? and How Should Different Prison Populations Be Treated? For better or for worse, governments turn to privately run prisons, as they turn to state-run prisons, in an effort to balance cost and safety, justice, and humanity.

CHAPTER 1

Are American Prisons Effective?

Chapter Preface

Imprisoning people is costly. The Florida Department of Corrections explained on its Web site that it cost $55.09 on average per day, or $20,108 per year to keep each inmate in prison. "Most of the daily cost . . . is spent on security and medical services," the Web site notes, with the rest spent on food, clothing, education, and administration. The total cost of corrections to the state is more than $2 billion, about 8.5 percent of the state's general revenue budget.

Florida, a populous state, is on the high end of spending, but most other states also spend heavily on prisons. For example, Pennsylvania spent $1.6 billion in 2007 on prisons, according to a March 9, 2008, article titled "In Your State: Prison Costs" on the Public Broadcasting Service (PBS) Web site. The same source showed Wisconsin spending $890 million in 2007 on prisons, Oklahoma spending $461 million, Texas spending almost $3.3. billion, and California spending a whopping $8.8 billion.

Money spent on prisons is, of course, money that cannot be spent elsewhere. In 2007, California spent eighty-three cents on prison for every dollar spent on higher education, according to the PBS article. New York spent seventy-three cents on prisons for every dollar on higher education. Fewer prisons could, therefore, mean more money for higher education or for other priorities.

For this reason, some advocates argue that the United States should try to move away from imprisonment and toward less costly forms of punishment. For instance, a study by Alison Lawrence sponsored by the National Conference of State Legislatures titled *Cutting Corrections: Earned Time Policies for State Prisoners* discussed a Washington State program where low-risk prisoners could earn time off their sentence through educational programs. An economist evaluating the program said that it saved taxpayers $5,500 per offender in prison costs, plus additional savings by reducing recidivism. There was also, however, an estimated loss due to the fact that some of the released prisoners would commit more crimes. Overall, balancing losses and gains, the economist concluded that there was a savings to taxpayers of $7,200 per offender.

The economic downturn that began in 2008 hit state budgets hard, and many states responded by closing prisons and locking up fewer people.

Some commentators, however, have been concerned that the rush to release prisoners may result in a threat to public safety. An editorial in the *Denver Post* on September 16, 2009, argued that an early parole program risked releasing some violent offenders as well as drug users, burglars, and other nonviolent offenders. The editorial noted, "Ultimately, it's the parole board's duty to protect Coloradans from violent offenders." As money becomes tighter, governments will continue to struggle to balance public safety with the cost of prisons in an effort to find a system of punishment that is both effective and cost-effective. The viewpoints in the following chapter debate how and whether this can be done.

Viewpoint 1

> *"Incarceration is a very effective method of deterring future victimization from those within our nation's jails and prisons."*

Prison Deters Crime

Bruce Bayley

Bruce Bayley is a former correctional officer and deputy juvenile probation officer who now is an associate professor of criminal justice at Weber State University in Utah and an adjunct instructor at Weber State Police Academy. In the following viewpoint, Bayley makes a distinction between general deterrence, in which the threat of prison broadly deters crime, and specific deterrence, in which individuals are sentenced to prison to incapacitate them and prevent them from committing more crimes. Bayley argues that prison is justified because it provides effective specific deterrence. General deterrence is of secondary concern, though Bayley suggests it may be effective as well in some cases.

As you read, consider the following questions:

1. According to Bayley, is the focus of general deterrence on the public or on the specific criminal?

Bruce Bayley, "Custody vs. Treatment Debate: Deterrence—The Two Great Lies," *CorrectionsOne*, July 1, 2009. Reproduced by permission of the author.

2. What is the second Great Lie of the deterrent debate, according to the author?
3. What does Bayley say is the primary job of incarceration?

Whenever the debate of imprisonment versus rehabilitation arises, the discussion turns to the concept of deterrence.

Those who believe in the virtues of rehabilitation frequently cite the "fact" that incarceration is not a deterrent to crime. This is what I call one of the two "Great Lies" in the treatment versus punishment debate.

To best understand these common lies, we need to first better define the term "deterrence" and recognize its purpose.

Deterrence refers to two distinct theoretical positions:

1. *General (or secondary) deterrence.* In the profession of corrections, those who believe in the value of general deterrence claim that criminal offenders' sentences discourage others in the community from committing similar crimes. For example, if someone is convicted of robbing a convenience store and sentenced to jail or prison, their punishment will cause others to think twice before committing a similar crime. Specifically, we call it general deterrence because the deterrent effect is designed to take place within the general public and not necessarily the individual who committed the crime.
2. *Specific (or primary) deterrence.* The second, and more relevant, concept of deterrence takes place through direct prevention. When an individual who has committed a crime is placed behind bars, they no longer are able to pursue crimes against society—period. For example, if someone is convicted of robbing a convenience store and sentenced to jail or prison, that specific person is separated from the general public and, thus, is no longer

More Prisoners, Less Crime

In the last 10 years, the effect of prison on crime rates has been studied by many scholars. . . . Among them is Steven Levitt. . . . He and others have shown that states that sent a higher fraction of convicts to prison had lower rates of crime, even after controlling for all of the other ways . . . that the states differed. A high risk of punishment reduces crime. Deterrence works.

But so does putting people in prison. The typical criminal commits from 12 to 16 crimes a year (not counting drug offenses). Locking him up spares society those crimes. Several scholars have separately estimated that the increase in the size of our prison population has driven down crime rates by 25%.

James Q. Wilson,
Los Angeles Times,
March 30, 2008.

a criminal threat to society. The purpose of the deterrent effect is simply to stop the specific offender from committing crimes and is not designed to cause any disincentive to the general public.

To summarize:

- Incarceration as a general or secondary deterrent discourages others from committing the same or similar behavior. The focus is on the general public and *not* the criminal.
- Incarceration as a specific or primary deterrent controls the offender from committing further crimes during the course of imprisonment. The focus is on a specific criminal and *not* the general public.

Prison Is a Specific Deterrent

The first Great Lie of the deterrence argument is that incarceration is not a deterrent.

When someone is sentenced to jail or prison, that individual is physically separated from society (the modern version of banishment—society's first form of punishment). In doing so, the person is *quite literally* deterred from committing any further crimes against the general public because (due to their incarceration) they simply no longer have physical access to the community.

Remember, a specific deterrent is not concerned about keeping others from committing crimes, but instead, focuses on preventing specific people who have violated the rules of society from victimizing the general public while they are imprisoned.

Is incarceration a deterrent? In this sense, yes—a specific deterrent.

General Deterrence Not the Goal

The next Great Lie of the deterrent debate centers on the belief that incarceration should act as a general deterrent. The truth is that it might, but it wasn't designed to do so.

The primary reason we sentence individuals to jail or prison is to punish them for the criminal offense(s) they have committed against society. If there are residual, or general, deterrent effects on other members of the community, that's great, but it's *not* the primary reason we incarcerate offenders.

Imagine sitting in a courtroom and hearing the judge say, "Well Mr. Smith, the jury has found you guilty and, to ensure others won't commit the same crime you did, you're being sentenced to one year in the county jail." Such a verdict would be absurd. There would be public outrage, lawsuits, and feelings of injustice throughout the community. This is why we incarcerate individuals to punish them, *not* to deter others.

The same general and specific deterrent effects discussed above also apply to rehabilitation. Whenever an offender enters any type of treatment, that particular individual is hopefully doing so for personal improvement—a specific deterrent. But when was the last time a rehabilitation program has been implemented or an individual has entered treatment simply to keep others from committing a criminal behavior?

The primary job of incarceration is to punish specific offenders for their crimes against society.

Don't let others tell you that confinement is not a deterrent. As discussed above, incarceration is a very effective method of deterring future victimization from those within our nation's jails and prisons.

As a specific deterrent, both imprisonment and rehabilitation have merit, but when addressing the aspects of general deterrence, ask yourself one simple question—which would be a greater deterrent for you as a member of society: prison or a treatment program?

"Studies . . . are calling into question whether either policing or punishment successfully deters crime."

Prison Does Not Deter Crime

Joel Waldfogel

Joel Waldfogel is the Ehrenkranz Family Professor of Business and Public Policy at the Wharton School of the University of Pennsylvania. In the following viewpoint, he reports on a Florida study in which researchers looked at whether crime rates among eighteen-year-olds who faced adult jail sentences differed from crime among seventeen-year-olds who faced lighter, juvenile sentences. The researchers found that the tougher sentences seemed to have no effect in deterring crime. However, Waldfogel notes, there was some evidence that putting specific criminals in jail for longer periods incapacitated those offenders and prevented them from committing as many crimes.

As you read, consider the following questions:

1. How do crime waves tend to affect policing and punishment in Waldfogel's view?

Joel Waldfogel, "The Irrational 18-Year-Old Criminal," *Slate*, www.washingtonpost.com, January 30, 2007.

2. What data did David S. Lee and Justin McCrary use to conduct their study, as reported by the author?
3. In the Lee and McCrary study, as cited by Waldfogel, what fraction of the people arrested after their eighteenth birthday were rearrested within a month?

Crime control is one of the oldest problems facing social science, dating at least to [Cesare] Beccaria, the 18th-century Italian philosopher who tried to put punishment on a rational footing. Two basic tools for controlling crime are policing and imprisonment, corresponding broadly to the first and second half-hours of a *Law & Order* episode. (In the vintage cast lineup, Detective Lennie Briscoe identifies a prime suspect before the second commercial break, and then prosecutor Jack McCoy does battle in court to get the defendant prison time.)

Testing Deterrence

Both the prospect of getting caught and the prospect of spending time in prison are supposed to deter forward-looking, rational potential offenders from criminal activity, encouraging more constructive pursuits like staying in school or at least making French fries. More mechanically, prison also prevents crime by simply caging dangerous people. Deterrence has long been an article of faith among economic theorists and, more recently, economists who do empirical work, too. But now a series of careful studies by economists at Columbia and the University of Michigan are calling into question whether either policing or punishment successfully deters crime.

With the traditional tools of social science, the deterrent effect of policing and punishment is hard to measure. Usually, empiricists infer an effect if crime is lower in circumstances with stiffer punishments or more policing. The problem is that tougher policies don't occur randomly. Cities and states add police or lengthen sentences as a frustrated response to

Certainty and Deterrence

The effectiveness of punishment relates to how far it is successful in suppressing the undesired behavior. . . .

Crucial seems to be the relationship between effectiveness and severity, in criminal justice this translates into whether certainty of apprehension is more effective than the severity of punishment. Clearly if there was a severe punishment but no one got caught, the likely effect on behavior change because of the punishment would be low. Alternatively, having a high certainty of getting caught with no consequences is not likely to prove effective (although, because of the apprehension effect, it still has some ability to depress the occurrence of unwanted behavior). An optimization of a low to moderate punishment combined with a moderate to high certainty of apprehension seems to be the most effective combination.

Stuart Henry,
Incarceration Nation conference,
October 24, 2003.

crime waves. So, crime affects policing and punishment as much as the other way around. This is one of the classic conundrums of empirical social science.

If social scientists ran the criminal justice system, it would be easy for them to measure the deterrent effect of longer sentences. They'd find a group of potential offenders and lengthen prison sentences the group would face if convicted. The scientists would make sure their target, likely delinquents, knew about the change, and then follow them and track whether they committed fewer offenses following the date their criminal penalties would increase.

In practice, of course, such an experiment, and the individual data needed to track it, aren't on offer. David S. Lee of Columbia and Justin McCrary of Michigan have surmounted this obstacle. The economists noted that when kids turn 18, they suddenly face much stiffer adult sanctions. Then they got access to data on all felony arrests in Florida between 1989 and 2002. Each arrest links to an individual, whose birth date is included in the data. This allowed the researchers to create an arrest history for each person arrested and to measure the effect of turning 18, and thus facing longer prison terms, on criminal activity.

In Florida during the years in question, Lee and McCrary found, the probability of being sentenced to prison for an offense jumped from 3 percent to 17 percent at exactly age 18. This tees up the answer to the economists' main question: How does the tendency to commit crimes vary around the 18th birthday, when the odds of a prison-sentence punishment jump? The answer is, hardly at all. While the probability of being arrested each week falls steadily from age 17 to age 19, there is no sizeable decrease in the arrest rate that corresponds to the bump up to an adult penalty in the weeks before and after people turn 18. To an economist, this is odd. At the grocery store, in weeks that Coke is on sale and Pepsi is not, consumers respond immediately. Coke sells out while Pepsi languishes on the shelf.

Evidence for Incapacitation

If the prospect of longer prison sentences does not deter young Floridians from committing crimes, prison still prevents some crime via the more mundane channel of locking them up—incapacitating rather than deterring them, in the lingo of criminal justice theory. Lee and McCrary see this in the rearrest data they study. One-fifth of the people arrested the week before their 18th birthday were rearrested within a month. By contrast, only a tenth of the people arrested a week *after* their 18th birthday were rearrested within the same time period. The reason? The 18-year-old offenders spent more of the month behind bars (because they received longer sentences, on average) and therefore were not free to commit the crimes that would have gotten them re-arrested.

The conclusion that prison time prevents crime through incapacitation rather than deterrence raises questions about the effect of policing. What benefit do cities and states get from putting more cops on the street? In earlier work, McCrary re-examined evidence about the relationship between police levels and crime in American cities, and concluded that existing data do not allow us to "learn about the causal effect of police on crime."

It would be premature to discard literally decades of scientific research based on one or two studies. Still, these studies should keep the debate going. It may be a while before we hear that *Law & Order* DUN-dun sound letting us know that the case is closed.

VIEWPOINT 3

> *"Punishment and rehabilitation can go together."*

Prisons Can Rehabilitate

Shreveport Times

The Shreveport Times *is a daily newspaper based in Shreveport, Louisiana. In the following viewpoint, the paper says that there are endemic substance abuse problems among Louisiana's prison population. The* Times *argues that by investing in rehabilitation programs in prison and by continuing care after prisoners are released, the state can save substantially by reducing reincarceration rates.*

As you read, consider the following questions:

1. According to the *Shreveport Times*, what percentage of Louisiana prisoners have substance abuse issues?
2. Of prisoners released in 2002, how many were back in prison by 2007, according to the author?
3. How many beds are designated for people in Caddo Correctional's "therapeutic community," according to the *Times*?

Periodically, a letter shows up in the programs office at Caddo Correctional Center [in Louisiana] declaring the jail's substance abuse treatment programs changed someone's life. A former prisoner is living clean and sober.

Other times, letters come from other Louisiana prisons asking for help. There, the prisoner doesn't have access to treatment programs but realizes he or she needs it.

About 80 percent of the inmates in Louisiana prisons have a substance abuse problem that contributed to their crimes: it could be possession of a large quantity, theft in order to buy more, or sometimes violent crime.

Treatment Can Help

It doesn't take much of a leap in logic to say treating substance abuse issues in prison could decrease crime and recidivism rates. Statistics abound:

- Of the 13,000 inmates in state prisons who have been identified as having a substance abuse problem, less than 7,000 are receiving treatment.
- 49 percent of inmates were high or intoxicated when they committed their crimes, according to a 2002 study.
- The same study found 82 percent of those in prison with addictions were nonviolent offenders.

Addiction is certainly no excuse for breaking the law, and even nonviolent criminals should be punished. But rehabilitation to prevent further, more serious crimes is also part of the Corrections Department's mission statement.

Several projects are in the works to add rehabilitation components to prisons, and they deserve the support of state government.

Representative Roy Burrell has two bills asking for studies of this very issue. And Caddo Sheriff Steve Prator hopes to expand his programs to the state prisoners held at Caddo Correctional.

"We are slowly realizing it doesn't help society to incarcerate without any rehabilitation," Burrell said.

The first of his studies, which is waiting on a Senate vote, would research providing substance abuse treatment in all jails and prisons in the state. We encourage lawmakers to approve the resolution.

His second study, already approved, will examine sentencing provisions that emphasize rehabilitation.

They rose out of concerns about overcrowded prisons and recidivism [reoffense and rearrest] rates. Of the prisoners released in 2002, half were back in prison by the end of 2007.

And of those who return with a new charge, 41 percent go back because of a drug-related crime.

To Michael Duffy, assistant secretary of the Office for Addictive Disorders, this is an easy place for his department to offer help. He has already launched a $13.4 million program to help prisoners re-enter society and maintain sobriety.

"We have a public health issue that we have not appropriately addressed, and it becomes a public safety issue."

A Model Program

Caddo Correctional offers one potentially model program. It has designated 78 beds for men enrolled in the "therapeutic community." It requires them to exercise as a group twice a week and attend group sessions four days a week. Once they complete the program, they can help facilitate for newcomers.

If they don't take it seriously or don't follow the rules, it's back to general population. The program has 115 names on a waiting list.

"We hope they can experience a different way of life," said David Boone, manager of inmate programs at Caddo Correctional. "We try to teach them how to deal with their emotions—shame, sadness, guilt."

Right now, all those prisoners are unsentenced, so the motivation to be involved could be more about getting a break

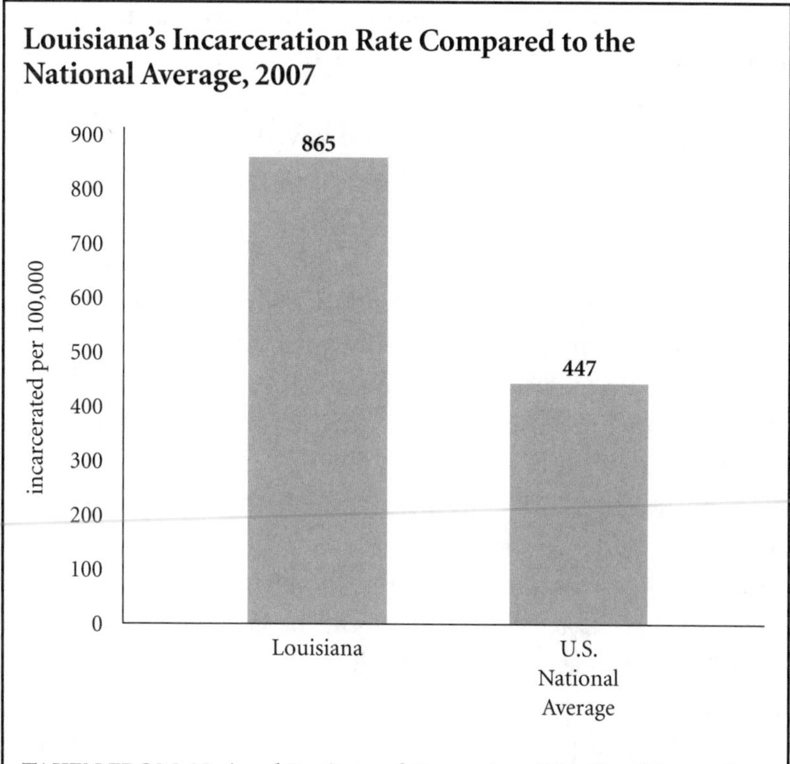

from a judge, but Boone is OK with that. He trusts that some of it sinks in and, if nothing else, those prisoners are better behaved than others.

Boone's next goal is to have a similar unit for the sentenced, state prisoners housed at the jail. While state prisons all have some sort of substance abuse program, the Corrections Department is looking into how many jails—which house 45 percent of state prisoners—offer the programs.

"I want to build something like nowhere else in the state," Boone said.

He envisions a place for the first-time, nonviolent drug offender where they could be sentenced to treatment and work release. That would also leave prison space open for violent criminals.

Corrections Secretary Jimmy LeBlanc isn't entirely sure about the practicalities of that sort of alternative sentencing but is convinced treatment prior to re-entry is critical. "We have those we will never fix, but we have those who never had the opportunity. I want to provide an opportunity."

Ongoing Support

The programs should also take into account the need for help once prisoners are released, whether through halfway houses, faith-based programs, or other nonprofits.

"You can have the finest treatment program behind bars, but this is a chronic, relapseable illness. And if you don't have support in place, it is extremely difficult to stay clean and sober," Duffy said.

These studies are the first step to getting the funding necessary to meet that goal. Both should be completed before the 2009 legislative session and should be full of compelling statistics that make the case for expanded treatment.

Will it be expensive? Probably, but it would be spending up front that would lead to long-term savings in trying and incarcerating repeat offenders.

With administration officials behind the effort, Burrell feels confident progress can be made on reform for prisoners and the system.

"[I] need to represent the people that sent me and do something that will fix something instead of put Band-Aids on it," he said.

Sadly, Louisiana has the highest incarceration rate in the country. We should at least have a model system that shows punishment and rehabilitation can go together.

Viewpoint 4

"While . . . there are no guarantees that rehabilitative programs will work, one thing that is *guaranteed is that a criminal in prison cannot commit violent crimes out on the streets."*

Prison Rehabilitation Efforts Are Ineffective

Dana Pico

Dana Pico is a conservative writer and blogger. In the following viewpoint, he argues that releasing prisoners early because they have completed rehabilitation programs may endanger the public. He points in particular to two police shootings in Philadelphia, both of which were committed by men who obtained early release through rehabilitation programs.

As you read, consider the following questions:

1. Who is William DiMascio, as reported by the author?
2. According to Pico, why did Judge Hamlin give Daniel Gidding the legal minimum sentence for his crime?
3. According to the author, what is the most important function of our prison system?

Dana Pico, "The Pennsylvania Prison Society: Advocating Exactly the Wrong Things," *Common Sense Political Thought*, June 16, 2009. Reproduced by permission of the author.

I've mentioned more than a few times that if our criminal justice system really did its job, there would be fewer murdered policemen in Philadelphia.

Well, on the op-ed page in [the June 16, 2009,] *Philadelphia Inquirer* comes the kind of thinking that just really, really fries me. William DiMascio, executive director of the Pennsylvania Prison Society, a prison reform advocacy group, makes about the worst comparison he could ever make [in an article titled "Longer Sentences Won't Stem Shootings"]:

> Pennsylvania's criminal justice system is in disarray, and the steps we are taking to address the problem offer little hope. . . .

Mr. DiMascio then proceeds to the worst example he could have used; it really left me shaking my head in astonishment:

> Philadelphia's recent spate of fatal police shootings were committed by former prisoners—partly the fruit of our punitive policies. Daniel Giddings, the 27-year-old parolee who killed police Officer Patrick McDonald, spent as much of his life in custody as on the streets.
>
> The violence of men like Giddings may not have been born inside prisons, but their years in the so-called corrections environment apparently did little to change them. These tragedies should raise questions not about how much time they served, but about what was done with them during that time. . . .

Rehabilitation Was Tried

Mr. DiMascio had complained that too many released prisoners left custody with no marketable skills. But it just so happens that Daniel Giddings, for whom Philadelphia Assistant District Attorney Joseph Coolican asked Common Pleas Court Judge Lynn B. Hamlin to impose the maximum possible sentence of 22½ to 45 years, and said that there was "absolutely no reason to believe" that it would ever be safe to release Mr. Giddings, was given the legal *minimum* sentence of 6 to 12 years, *for an armed robbery in which he shot the victim in the knees*, because Judge Hamlin was impressed by his grades in finishing a high school diploma while in custody.

If Judge Hamlin had not been impressed by Mr. Giddings doing just what Mr. DiMascio said was not provided enough for prisoners, and had listened to Mr. Coolican's impassioned plea for a maximum sentence, Mr. Giddings *would still have been in prison on the day he killed Officer McDonald!*

Op-ed writers are frequently not the ones who write the article titles; it is entirely possible the the editorial staff of the *Inquirer* assigned Mr. DiMascio's article the title "Longer Sentences Won't Stem Shootings." But the example given is one in which a longer sentence *would* have prevented a shooting.

Mr. DiMascio continues with flawed logic:

> The latest example of our reactionary, crisis-by-crisis policymaking is a state House bill portrayed as requiring prison without parole for repeat violent offenders. . . .
>
> Under the bill, Pennsylvania judges would be required to impose sentences of 15 to 30 years for a second violent offense—up from 10 to 20 years under current law—followed by 15 years of intensive post-prison supervision. A third violent offense would get a flat sentence of at least 30 and as much as life.
>
> This would provide little incentive for anyone in prison to behave, much less bother trying to improve. . . .

What Mr. DiMascio has forgotten is the concept of time. If a second violent offense will net a man a 15 to 30 year sentence, even if he gets out after the minimum 15 years, assuming that he was convicted at age 20, he'll be 35 by the time he gets out, the time he is starting to pull out of his most violent years. A third violent offense, now with a minimum 30 year sentence, incarcerates the criminal until he is at least 65 years old. By that time, the vast majority of such men are well beyond their most violent years, and, being elderly, are probably much weakened physically.

While Mr. DiMascio admits that there are no guarantees that rehabilitative programs will work, one thing that *is* guaranteed is that a criminal in prison cannot commit violent crimes out on the streets.

The sad part about the whole thing is that we have tried it Mr. DiMascio's way. That's how Mr. Giddings was able to earn his GED [general education development degree] while in custody, and that's why Judge Hamlin sentenced Mr. Giddings to a minimum sentence.

Mercy Should Not Trump Justice

And the killing of Officer McDonald was, sadly, not an isolated incident where a criminal was treated leniently. Philadelphia Police Officer Charles Cassidy was killed by John Lewis. Mr. Lewis had a robbery charge dismissed because he completed a drug treatment program, even though that robbery was committed *after* his arrest and admission into that drug treatment program. The criminal justice system tried to provide Mr. Lewis with a rehabilitation program—rehabilitation from drugs, in this instance—just as Mr. DiMascio believes ought to be done, and Mr. Lewis was left out on the street long enough to kill a police officer.

The . . . banner for the Pennsylvania Prison Society, from their website, [shows] children, whom I suppose we are to assume are the children of the prisoners, children unable to have their fathers at home because they are incarcerated, and the site does indicate programs to help children so situated.

But what strikes me is their slogan, "Justice and Compassion since 1787." Too often it has seemed that, in showing

Saga of Daniel Giddings

In his first encounter with the criminal-justice system in 1991, Daniel Giddings was convicted of beating and robbing a mentally disabled man in his North Philadelphia neighborhood.

Giddings was 10 years old. . . .

About a month after Giddings was released from prison to a halfway house, the 27-year-old man died in a shoot-out after police said he gunned down Officer Patrick McDonald following a traffic stop. Police say Giddings delivered the fatal shots while the wounded officer lay on a North Philadelphia street.

Andrew Maykuth and Dwight Ott,
Philadelphia Inquirer, *June 30, 2009.*

compassion, justice has not been done—and much more *in*justice gets done to the innocent people in a society into which criminals are too easily released.

In the end, Mr. DiMascio's article fails because he has listed the choices incorrectly. In his article, Mr. DiMascio presents our incarceration policies as choices between punishment and rehabilitation. Unfortunately, he has ignored the most important function of our prison system, the function on which most people concentrate: the protection of society from criminals. Sensible citizens want the truly violent criminals locked away to protect society from their violence. That is the truly important point, and it is the one Mr. DiMascio completely missed.

Viewpoint 5

> *"In a country with the world's largest prison population . . . alternate punishments are now a . . . necessity."*

Alternative Sentencing Would Be More Effective Than Prison

Ruth David

Ruth David is an India correspondent for Forbes. *In the following viewpoint, she suggests that various alternative programs could reduce the reliance on expensive prisons. Among the suggestions she highlights are drug treatment programs, breathalyzers in the cars of repeat drunk drivers to prevent them from driving under the influence, chemical castration for child molesters, and inner-city teaching appointments for corporate criminals.*

As you read, consider the following questions:

1. Which offenses does the U.S. Justice Department define as violent crimes, according to the author?
2. How much higher is the murder rate in Chicago than the national average, according to David?

Ruth David, "Ten Alternatives to Prison," Forbes.com, April 16, 2006.

3. Which was the first state to pass chemical castration laws for repeat child molesters, as reported by the author?

Country singer Johnny Cash immortalized inmates' miseries in his classic song "Folsom Prison Blues." But now, as slammers across the country run out of space and resources, prison officials are feeling pretty blue as well.

Nobody likes these expensive, ugly messes, so why not explore alternate punishments that keep people out of lockup?

Innovative Programs

The choices range from probation to public shaming. For drunken driving convictions, some offenders have been made to drive around with signs pasted on the vehicles declaring they've been convicted. Others have been ordered to install Breathalyzer devices that prevent a vehicle from starting if the driver has been drinking.

Legal experts suggest the skills of corporate criminals could be used to offset rising costs in state prisons. "I personally feel we should have a program that lets corporate criminals go to low-income schools and teach," says Stephen Saltzburg, chairman of the American Bar Association's Task Force on Effective Criminal Sanctions. This should be combined with hefty fines for corporate criminals, he says, and schools should seek parents' approval before unleashing criminals on their children in the classroom.

For minors in danger of landing in prison, there might be no better cure than a heart-to-heart talk with convicts. The In My Shoes program in Chicago tries to ensure these adolescents never need to step into the shoes of those who've walked the road to prison.

Prison still seems to be the best bet for violent crimes, defined by the U.S. Justice Department as homicide, rape, rob-

Positive Results From CeaseFire Outreach

Community	Policing Beat	Shootings Before Implementation	2007 Shootings	Change Since Implementation (by beat)	Change Since Implementation (by community)
Auburn Gresham	611	26	16	–38.5%	–46.3%
	612	28	13	–53.6%	
	1111	31	8	–74.2%	–72.5%
11th District	1112	44	15	–65.9%	
	1121	34	7	–79.4%	
Logan Square	1413	26	4	–84.6%	–88.0%
	2525	24	2	–91.7%	
Humboldt Park	1422	8	8	0.0%	–50.0%
	1423	12	2	–83.3%	
Total		233	75	–67.8%	

The neighborhoods in the chart were selected for outreach and intervention by CeaseFire, an initiative of the Project for Violence Prevention in Chicago.

TAKEN FROM: CeaseFire: The Campaign to Stop the Shooting Web Site, "2008 Annual Report", 2008.

bery, and assault. And with a prison population of over 2.1 million, the U.S. relies heavily on prison time to punish criminals and prevent crime.

Of course, the prevention part doesn't seem to be working very well. A 2002 federal study tracked inmates for three years after their release from state prisons in 1994 and found that 67% committed a crime within the next three years.

The Brooklyn, New York, district attorney's office is one of the state bodies working on alternatives aimed at reducing high recidivism rates. District Attorney Charles Hynes says the office's star program, Drug Treatment Alternatives-to-Prison, took off after it was redesigned to specifically target second-felony offenders. "When faced with the prospect of mandatory jail time, offenders do not oppose rehab," he says. Statistics show that those who complete the program are three and a half times likelier to get a job than they were before their arrest. And it costs half of what prison time would.

Several other initiatives targeted at keeping people out of prison or ensuring they don't return are community-based, and this is considered crucial to their success. Assistant District Attorney Anne Swern says community-based efforts have helped slash crime rates in Brooklyn, where index crimes—the FBI's most serious crimes—declined by 74% since 1990. And thanks to reduced crime, real estate is booming in the area.

Not everyone is sold on these ideas. Alternatives to prison are workable only in a limited number of cases, and proposed sentences need to adhere to the federal sentencing guidelines, says U.S. District Judge John Keenan. His alternatives usually are community service and probation.

But in a country with the world's largest prison population, and where some states, like California, are accused of devoting more resources on the upkeep of criminals than on education—alternate punishments are now a question of necessity.

From Treatment to Teaching

Drug Treatment Alternatives-To-Prison. This program, started in October 1990, targets nonviolent drug addicts with previous convictions. Those who qualify enter a guilty plea and get a deferred sentence that allows them to enroll in a residential drug-treatment program, which ranges from 15 to 24 months. Addicts who successfully complete the program have their charges dismissed. But if they don't make it through, they are taken back to court and sentenced to prison time. Brooklyn District Attorney Charles Hynes, who initiated the project, said its graduates were 87% less likely than others to return to prison. The pioneering initiative is now run in at least 15 counties across New York State.

Faith-Based Rehabilitation Programs (InnerChange Freedom Initiative). Several states across the country have programs that use religious counselors from the community to help prisoners on their journey out of jail. In 1997, the Texas Department of Criminal Justice and Prison Fellowship, an international nonprofit prison ministry, launched what is believed to be the first such comprehensive effort. The program offers education, work life skills, and mentoring, but religious instruction is the crux of the effort. Many of these programs cater to Christian prisoners, but some also include Jews and Muslims.

Pay For Your Prison Stay. In 1996, jails in Missouri, Connecticut, and New Mexico began charging inmates for their room and board. Three years before that, Congress approved legislation to allow the Federal Bureau of Prisons to collect user fees from inmates to cover the cost of their incarceration. Prisoners pay anywhere between $8 and $65 or more for segregated cells and marginally better food and lodging.

The Project For Violence Prevention (Chicago). Yes, we spent our childhoods hearing that prevention is better than cure. But physician Gary Slutkin wanted to reiterate that message to high-crime, gang-ridden neighborhoods in Chicago, which has a murder rate approximately four times the national average. Starting in 1995, Slutkin worked with small teams to build on existing alliances in the worst-hit neighborhoods. People who had lived in these neighborhoods formed outreach teams to interact with juveniles in danger of landing in prison. The University of Illinois' School of Public Health, a violence management team under Slutkin, monitors shootings throughout Chicago on a 24-hour basis. When a shooting is reported, project members from the neighborhood and churches gather at the scene to express their disapproval, through rallies, setting up monuments or prayer services.

Classes And Fees: For The Rich. This isn't a reality yet. But how about letting corporate criminals teach in low-income schools? Plenty of them have been educated at the finest of schools, so why should they just sit around gazing out their prison windows on the taxpayers' dime? asks Stephen Saltzburg, chairman of the American Bar Association's Task Force on Effective Criminal Sanctions. Of course unlike regular teachers, participants in this program would be escorted to school and back to ensure they don't skip class.

From Breathalyzers to Billboards

Ignition Interlocks. Judges in states including Maryland and California have made drunken drivers install Breathalyzer devices in their vehicles. The ignition interlocks prevent the vehicle from starting until the driver blows into the mouthpiece, and the device confirms he or she hasn't been drinking.

Live In Slummy Buildings. In February 1988, a Brooklyn, N.Y., landlord found guilty of keeping his tenants in appalling conditions was sentenced to spend 15 days in his building, in the freezing cold and alongside leaky pipes and rats. He had to wear an electronic ankle cuff that ensured he didn't stray beyond a 100-foot radius. The sentence was later popularized in a 1991 motion picture, *The Super*. Today, such sentences are not unusual across the country.

Chemical Castration. In 1996, California became the first state to pass a law requiring chemical castration for repeat child molesters. The procedure is noninvasive and reversible. Offenders are usually injected once every three months with a drug called Depo-Provera, which inhibits hormones that stimulate the production of testosterone, eliminating sex drive. Once offenders stop taking the drug, their sex drive returns to normal. At least nine states, including Florida, Georgia, Oregon, and Texas, now have chemical castration laws in place.

Abolish Prisons! Invest The Money In People. It may sound like a radical idea. But locking people up in cages doesn't make society safer, says Rose Braz, director of Critical Resistance, a national grassroots group that works to abolish prisons. So why not try something different? "Our goal is to create safer communities. The way to do that is for the government to invest in housing, education, and job training. We know that communities where these needs are met have lower crime rates," says Rose.

The Restorative Justice program, a community-based program run by the Department of Corrections in Minnesota, actively involves the victim in . . . deciding an aggressor's punishment. The program works with trained mediators to facilitate meetings between the victim and aggressor, and gives offenders a chance to voluntarily apologize and explain their actions. Reparation can take the form of financial payments, going to work for the victim or community service. Restorative Justice programs rely largely on voluntary cooperation from all those involved in a crime. If neither party is willing, formal justice takes its course.

The Billboard Project. This isn't the kind of billboard fame you'd want to court. In a bid to shame men into stayinq away from prostitutes, an association in Omaha, Nebraska, began a project to put their names and faces on billboards. In October 2003, the first of its kind billboard went up, warning men that if they were convicted of soliciting prostitutes, they would see their names on the board. The community-based initiative began with a grant of $2,500 from a neighborhood group.

VIEWPOINT 

"Just how do you 'supervise' a criminal who is turned loose in the community? Assigning someone to be with him, one on one and 24/7, would probably be a lot more expensive than locking him up."

Alternatives to Prison Are Dangerous and Ineffective

Thomas Sowell

Thomas Sowell is a senior fellow at the Hoover Institution at Stanford University. In the following viewpoint, he argues that high imprisonment rates reduce crime. On the other hand, Sowell maintains, alternatives to imprisonment allow criminals to threaten society. Sowell argues that supporters of alternative programs manipulate statistics to make the programs look successful when they are actually failures.

As you read, consider the following questions:

1. According to the *New York Times*, as cited by the author, what states spent as much or more on prison as on higher education?

Thomas Sowell, "Alternatives to Incarceration and the Costs of Crime," *Capitalism Magazine*, March 11, 2008. By permission Thomas Sowell and Creators Syndicate, Inc.

2. According to Sowell, what is the cost of imprisonment in Britain as compared to the cost of crimes committed by criminals?
3. What does the author say are some of the problems with electronic monitoring devices?

For more than two centuries, the political left has been preoccupied with the fate of criminals, often while ignoring or downplaying the fate of the victims of those criminals. So it is hardly surprising that a recent *New York Times* editorial has returned to a familiar theme among those on the left, on both sides of the Atlantic, with its lament that "incarceration rates have continued to rise while crime rates have fallen."

Prisons Reduce Crime

Back in 1997, *New York Times* writer Fox Butterfield expressed the same lament under the headline, "Crime Keeps on Falling, But Prisons Keep on Filling." Then, as now, liberals seemed to find it puzzling that crime rates go down when more criminals are put behind bars. Nor is it surprising that the left uses an old and irrelevant comparison—between the cost of keeping a criminal behind bars versus the cost of higher education. According to the *Times*, "Vermont, Connecticut, Delaware, Michigan, and Oregon devote as much or more to corrections as they do to higher education."

The relevant comparison would be between the cost of keeping a criminal behind bars and the cost of letting him loose in society. But neither the *New York Times* nor others on the left show any interest in that comparison. In Britain, the total cost of the prison system per year was found to be 1.9 billion pounds sterling, while the financial cost alone of the crimes committed per year by criminals was estimated at 60 billion pounds sterling.

Alternatives Fail in UK

The evidence for the failure of community penalties to stop crime and for the success of prisons in doing so is now so clear that there is no longer any rational argument left in this issue. . . . The savings to be accrued from imprisoning large numbers of criminals, who are therefore prevented from committing crime, are considerable, and too obvious for justice officials not to be aware of them. . . . We are left with the possibility that what drives these [lenient and alternative] ideas is ideology. It is certainly true of Britain that many of our policies, both in the field of criminal justice and elsewhere reflect the left-wing world view of those that promote them, and have little or nothing to do with an objective view of what the country needs to protect it from criminals.

David Fraser, New Zealand Fit for Criminals? *June 8, 2008. http://landfitforcriminals.org.nz.*

The big difference between the two kinds of costs is not just in their amounts. The cost of locking up criminals has to be paid out of government budgets that politicians would prefer to spend on giveaway programs that are more likely to get them re-elected. But the far higher costs of letting criminals loose is paid by the general public in both money and in being subjected to violence. The net result is that both politicians and ideologues of the left are forever pushing "alternatives to incarceration." These include programs with lovely names like "community supervision" and high-tech stuff like electronic devices to keep track of released criminals' locations.

Alternatives Do Not Work

Just how do you "supervise" a criminal who is turned loose in the community? Assigning someone to be with him, one on one and 24/7, would probably be a lot more expensive than locking him up.

But of course no one is proposing any such thing. Having the released criminal reporting to some official from time to time may be enough to allow the soothing word "supervision" to be used. But it hardly restricts what a criminal does with the other nine-tenths of his time when he is not reporting. Electronic devices work only when they are being used. Even when they are being used 24/7, they tell you only where the criminal is, not what he is doing. Those released criminals who don't even want that much restriction can of course remove the device and become an escapee, with far less trouble or risk than is required to escape from prison.

One of the most insidious aspects of "alternatives to incarceration" programs is that those who control such programs often control also the statistical and other information that would be needed to assess the actual consequences of these programs. They not only control what information is released but to whom it will be released. When officials whose careers are on the line can choose between researchers who view incarceration as being "mean-spirited" toward criminals and other researchers who are much less sympathetic to criminals, who do you think is going to get access to the data?

A study of the treatment of criminals in Britain—"A Land Fit for Criminals" by David Fraser—has several chapters on the games that are played with statistics, in order to make "alternatives to incarceration" programs look successful, even when they are failing abysmally, with tragic results for the public. Britain has gone much further down the road that the *New York Times* is urging us to follow. In the process, Britain has gone from being one of the most law-abiding nations on earth to overtaking the United States in most categories of crime.

Periodical Bibliography

The following articles have been selected to supplement the diverse views presented in this chapter.

Economist	"A Nation of Jailbirds," April 2, 2009.
Economist	"No More Room, No More Money," March 21, 2009.
Newton Frazer	"The Effects of Punishment to Deter Crime," *www.prisoners.com.*
David Green	"Crime Is Falling—Because Prison Works," *Guardian* (UK), July 20, 2003.
Aleks Kajstura, Peter Wagner, and William Goldberg	"The Geography of Punishment: How Huge Sentencing Enhancement Zones Harm Communities, Fail to Protect Children," *Prison Policy Initiative*, July 2008. www.prisonpolicy.org.
Laura Kurgan	"Prison Blocks," *Atlantic Monthly*, March 2009.
Eli Lehrr	"California's Prison Problem," *National Review Online*, August 5, 2009. http://corner.nationalreview.com.
Glenn Loury and Heather Mac Donald	"Social Science in the City," Bloggingheads, March 28, 2009. www.bloggingheads.tv.
Heather Mac Donald	"The Jail Inferno," *City Journal*, Summer 2009.
Tom McNichol	"Prison Cell-Phone Use a Growing Problem," *Time*, May 26, 2009.
Solomon Moore	"Prison Spending Outpaces All but Medicaid," *New York Times*, March 2, 2009.
James Q. Wilson	"Do the Time, Lower the Crime," *Los Angeles Times*, March 30, 2008.

Chapter 2

Are American Prisons Just?

Chapter Preface

In most of the United States, prostitution, or the sale of sex, is considered a crime and may be punished by jail or prison time.

Some critics have argued that treating prostitution as a crime is unjust. For instance, the Web site of the Decriminalize Prostitution Now Coalition argues that "people in a free society have the right to work in their chosen profession, and to do with their own bodies as they so choose. Likewise, all citizens have the right to engage in consensual adult sexual contact." An article in the *Economist* in October 2008 points out that legalizing prostitution might help protect prostitutes, who might otherwise be afraid to go to the police when abused by a customer or by their employers (often called pimps).

Some commentators have argued that prostitution should be illegal, but that the focus of enforcement should not be on the women but on the men (or johns) who purchase their services. According to the National Institute for Justice in an article on its Web site titled "Reducing Demand for Prostitution," currently in the United States, "Most arrests associated with prostitution are arrests of the women; about 10 percent are arrests of the men who purchase commercial sex."

Some jurisdictions are actively trying to reduce prostitution by focusing on those who solicit sex. One example is discussed in an August 27, 2009, post on the blog Music City Syndicate. According to the post, authorities in Nashville have started encouraging johns to attend education programs taught by health experts, former prostitutes, and law enforcement officers. Stephanie Davis, a policy advisor to the Atlanta mayor's office, is quoted as explaining that such programs are intended to show the johns that "this is not a victimless crime, and they are contributing to the exploitation of women. . . .

It's hurting them, the [men], and it's hurting their families, and it's hurting the community."

Finally, some commentators argue that to be just and compassionate, society must take a stand against both prostitutes and johns. Dorn Checkley, the director of WholeHearted, a project of the Pittsburgh Coalition Against Pornography, argued in an article on the organization's Web site that "prostitutes themselves are not evil and neither are their johns. They are usually broken and needy individuals seemingly trapped by the circumstances of their lives. Ultimately, to accept and legitimize prostitutes and johns is not compassionate, it is lazy. Not to undertake the difficult task of leading, encouraging and calling them to the higher way is a failure to love as Jesus would have loved them."

The arguments around prostitution are echoed in other areas of the debate about prison. What crimes are deserving of punishment? Who should be held responsible? What punishments are appropriate, and does compassion require us to reduce punishments or to enforce them strictly? All of these questions come up repeatedly when trying to determine how the U.S. prison system can become more just, as the arguments presented in the following viewpoints attest.

Viewpoint 1

> *"[America has] become a nation of jailers and, arguably, racist jailers at that."*

America's Imprisonment Practices Are Racist

Glenn Loury

Glenn Loury is the Merton P. Stoltz Professor of the Social Sciences at Brown University. In the following viewpoint, he asserts that America is exceptional in the number of people it imprisons. Loury argues that large imprisonment rates, and particularly the extremely high imprisonment rates of minorities, are linked to America's racist history. Loury says that social inequality breeds crime, which is then harshly punished. He contends that American society must rectify this issue by working to include marginalized groups and to end social injustice.

As you read, consider the following questions:

1. According to the author, how many of the world's inmates are housed in the United States?
2. According to Loury, what is the black-to-white male incarceration rate?

3. What does Leo Tolstoy identify as the core of Christianity, according to the author?

Imprisonment on a massive scale has become one of the central aspects of our nation's social policy toward the poor, powerfully impairing the lives of some of the most marginal of our fellow citizens, especially the poorly educated black and Hispanic men who reside in large numbers in our great urban centers.

The bare facts of this matter—concerning both the scale of incarceration and its racial disparity—have been much remarked upon of late. Simply put, we have become a nation of jailers and, arguably, racist jailers at that. The past four decades have witnessed a truly historic expansion, and transformation, of penal institutions in the United States—at every level of government, and in all regions of the country. We have, by any measure, become a vastly more punitive society. Measured in constant dollars and taking account of all levels of government, spending on corrections and law enforcement in the United States has more than quadrupled over the last quarter century. As a result, the American prison system has grown into a leviathan unmatched in human history. This development should be deeply troubling to anyone who professes to love liberty.

World's Leading Jailer

Here, as in other areas of social policy, the United States is a stark international outlier, sitting at the most rightward end of the political spectrum: We imprison at a far higher rate than the other industrial democracies—higher, indeed, than either Russia or China, and vastly higher than any of the countries of Western Europe. According to the International Centre for Prison Studies in London, there were in 2005 some 9 million prisoners in the world; more than 2 million were being held in the United States. With approximately one twentieth of the world's population, America had nearly one fourth of the world's inmates. At more than 700 per 100,000 residents, the U.S. incarceration rate was far greater than our nearest competitors (the Bahamas, Belarus, and Russia, which each have a rate of about 500 per 100,000.) Other industrial societies, some of them with big crime problems of their own, were less punitive than we by an order of magnitude: the United States incarcerated at 6.2 times the rate of Canada, 7.8 times the rate of France, and 12.3 times the rate of Japan.

The demographic profile of the inmate population has also been much discussed. In this, too, the U.S. is an international outlier. African Americans and Hispanics, who taken together are about one fourth of the population, account for about two thirds of state prison inmates. Roughly one third of state prisoners were locked up for committing violent offenses, with the remainder being property and drug offenders. Nine in ten are male, and most are impoverished. Inmates in state institutions average fewer than eleven years of schooling.

The extent of racial disparity in imprisonment rates exceeds that to be found in any other arena of American social life: at eight to one, the black to white ratio of male incarceration rates dwarfs the two to one ratio of unemployment rates, the three to one non-marital child bearing ratio, the two to one ratio of infant mortality rates and the one to five ratio of net worth. More black male high school dropouts are in prison than belong to unions or are enrolled in any state or federal social welfare programs. The brute fact of the matter is that the primary contact between black American young adult men and their government is via the police and the penal apparatus. Coercion is the most salient feature of their encounters with the state. According to estimates compiled by sociologist Bruce Western, nearly 60% of black male dropouts born between 1965 and 1969 had spent at least one year in prison before reaching the age of 35.

For these men, and the families and communities with which they are associated, the adverse effects of incarceration will extend beyond their stays behind bars. My point is that this is not merely law enforcement policy. It is social policy writ large. And no other country in the world does it quite like we do.

Cost of Prisoners

This is far more than a technical issue—entailing more, that is, than the task of finding the most efficient crime control policies. Consider, for instance, that it is not possible to conduct a cost-benefit analysis of our nation's world-historic prison buildup over the past 35 years without implicitly specifying how the costs imposed on the persons imprisoned, and their families, are to be reckoned. Of course, this has not stopped analysts from pronouncing on the purported net benefits to "society" of greater incarceration without addressing that question! Still, how—or, indeed, whether—to weigh the costs born by law-breakers—that is, how (or whether) to acknowledge their humanity—remains a fundamental and difficult question of social ethics. Political discourses in the United States have given insufficient weight to the collateral damage imposed by punishment policies on the offenders themselves, and on those who are knitted together with offenders in networks of social and psychic affiliation.

Whether or not one agrees, two things should be clear: social scientists can have no answers for the question of what weight to put on a "thug's," or his family's, well-being; and a morally defensible public policy to deal with criminal offenders cannot be promulgated without addressing that question. To know whether or not our criminal justice policies comport with our deepest values, we must ask how much additional cost borne by the offending class is justifiable per marginal unit of security, or of peace of mind, for the rest of us. This question is barely being asked, let alone answered, in the contemporary debate.

Nor is it merely the scope of the mass imprisonment state that has expanded so impressively in the United States. The ideas underlying the doing of criminal justice—the superstructure of justifications and rationalizations—have also undergone a sea change. Rehabilitation is a dead letter; retribution is the thing. The function of imprisonment is not to reform or redirect offenders. Rather, it is to keep *them* away from *us*. "The prison," writes sociologist David Garland, "is used today as a kind of reservation, a quarantine zone in which purportedly dangerous individuals are segregated in the name of public safety." We have elaborated what are, in effect, a "string of work camps and prisons strung across a vast country housing millions of people drawn mainly from classes and racial groups that are seen as politically and economically problematic." We have, in other words, marched quite a long way down the punitive road, in the name of securing public safety and meting out to criminals their just deserts.

And we should be ashamed of ourselves for having done so. Consider a striking feature of this policy development, one that is crucial to this moral assessment: the ways in which we now deal with criminal offenders in the United States have evolved in recent decades in order to serve expressive and not only instrumental ends. We have wanted to "send a message," and have done so with a vengeance. Yet in the process we have also, in effect, provided an answer for the question: who is to blame for the maladies that beset our troubled civilization? That is, we have constructed a narrative, created scapegoats, assuaged our fears, and indulged our need to feel virtuous about ourselves. We have met the enemy and the enemy, in the now familiar caricature, is *them*—a bunch of anomic [lawless], menacing, morally deviant "thugs." In the midst of this dramaturgy—unavoidably so in America—lurks a potent racial subplot.

This issue is personal for me. As a black American male, a baby-boomer born and raised on Chicago's South Side, I can

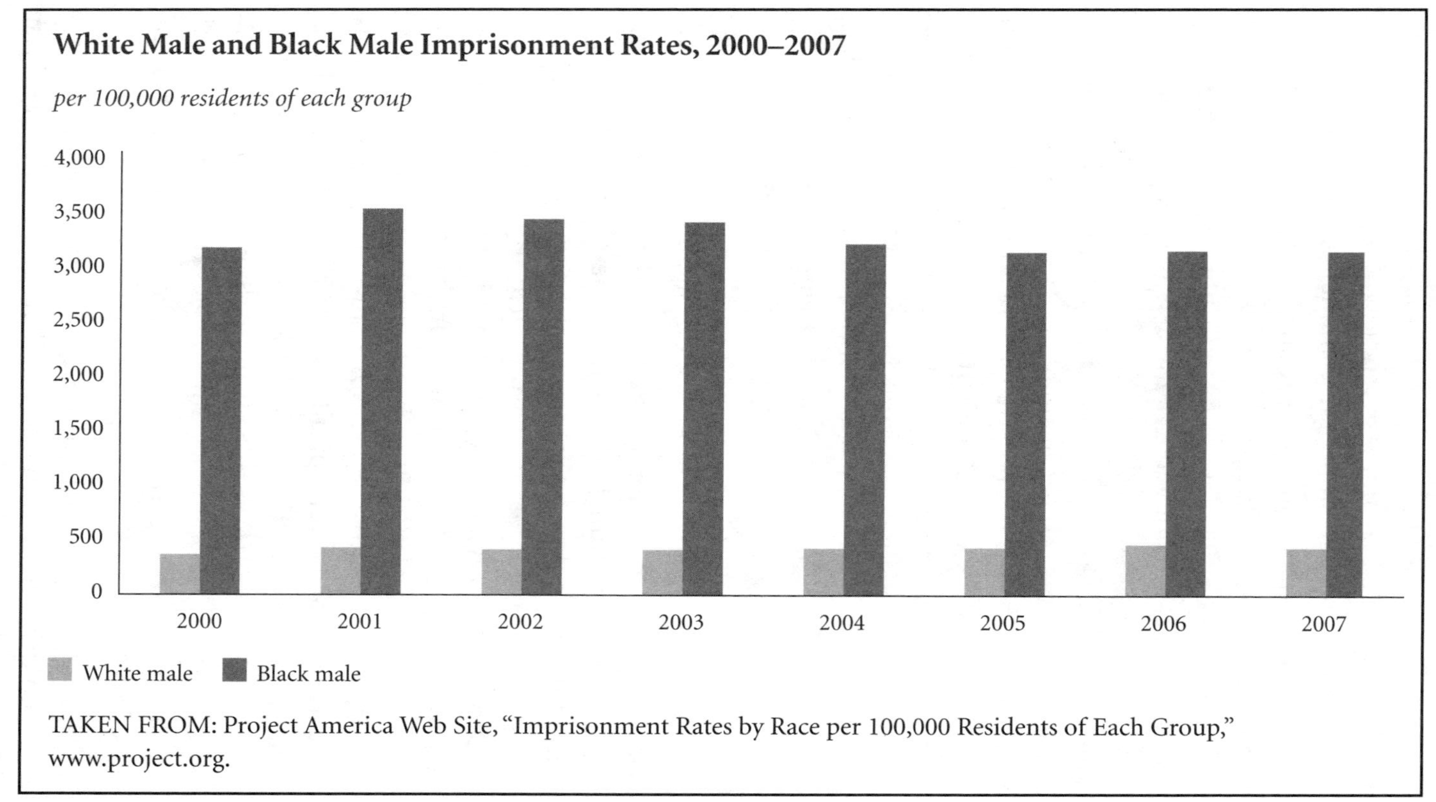

TAKEN FROM: Project America Web Site, "Imprisonment Rates by Race per 100,000 Residents of Each Group," www.project.org.

ocial Responsibility

his situation raises a moral problem that we cannot avoid. e cannot pretend that there are more important problems in r society, or that this circumstance is the necessary solution other, more pressing problems—unless we are also pre- ed to say that we have turned our backs on the ideal of lity for all citizens and abandoned the principles of jus- We ought to be asking ourselves two questions: Just what ner of people are we Americans? And in light of this, are our obligations to our fellow citizens—even those reak our laws?

ithout trying to make a full-fledged philosophical argu- ere, I nevertheless wish to gesture . . . toward some an- o these questions. I will not set forth a policy manifesto time. What I aim to do is suggest, in a general way, ought to be thinking differently about this problem. lly, given our nation's history and political culture, I t there are severe limits to the applicability in this nce of a pure ethic of personal responsibility, as the distributing the negative good of punishment in con- America. I urge that we shift the boundary toward knowledgment of social responsibility in our pun- licy discourse—even for wrongful acts freely cho- ividual persons. In suggesting this, I am not so ng a "root causes" argument—he did the crime, cause he had no choice—as I am arguing that the rge is implicated in his choices because we have structural arrangements which work to our ben- etriment, and yet which shape his consciousness identity. . . . I approach this problem of moral emphasizing that closed and bounded social e racially homogeneous urban ghettos—create e "pathological" and "dysfunctional" cultural but these forms are not intrinsic to the people

identify with the plight of the urban poor because I have lived among them. I am related to them by the bonds of social and psychic affiliation. As it happens, I have myself passed through the courtroom, and the jailhouse, on my way along life's journey. I have sat in the visitor's room at a state prison; I have known, personally and intimately, men and women who lived their entire lives with one foot to either side of the law. Whenever I step to a lectern to speak about the growth of imprisonment in our society, I envision voiceless and despairing people who would have me speak on their behalf. Of course, personal biography can carry no authority to compel agreement about public policy. Still, I prefer candor to the false pretense of clinical detachment and scientific objectivity. I am not running for high office; I need not pretend to a cool neutrality that I do not possess. While I recognize that these revelations will discredit me in some quarters, this is a fate I can live with.

Prisons Not Color-blind

So, my racial identity is not irrelevant to my discussion of the subject at hand. But, then, neither is it irrelevant that among the millions now in custody and under state supervision are to be found a vastly disproportionate number of the black and the brown. There is no need to justify injecting race into this discourse, for prisons are the most race-conscious public institutions that we have. No big city police officer is "color-blind" nor, arguably, can any afford to be. Crime and punishment in America have a color—just turn on a television, or open a magazine, or listen carefully to the rhetoric of a political campaign—and you will see what I mean. The fact is that, in this society as in any other, order is maintained by the threat and the use of force. We enjoy our good lives because we are shielded by the forces of law and order upon which we rely to keep the unruly at bay. Yet, in this society to an extent unlike virtually any other, those bearing the heavy burden of order-enforcement belong, in numbers far exceeding their presence in the population at large, to racially defined and historically marginalized groups. Why should this be so? And how can those charged with the supervision of our penal apparatus sleep well at night knowing that it is so?

This punitive turn in the nation's social policy is intimately connected, I would maintain, with public rhetoric about responsibility, dependency, social hygiene, and the reclamation of public order. And such rhetoric, in turn, can be fully grasped only when viewed against the backdrop of America's often ugly and violent racial history: There is a reason why our inclination toward forgiveness and the extension of a second chance to those who have violated our behavioral strictures is so stunted, and why our mainstream political discourses are so bereft of self-examination and searching social criticism. An historical resonance between the stigma of race and the stigma of prison has served to keep alive in our public culture the subordinating social meanings that have always been associated with blackness. Many historians and political scientists—though, of course, not all—agree that the shifting character of race relations over the course of the nineteenth and twentieth centuries helps to explain why the United States is exceptional among democratic industrial societies in the severity of its punitive policy and the paucity of its social-welfare institutions. Put directly and without benefit of euphemism, the racially disparate incidence of punishment in the United States is a morally troubling residual effect of the nation's history of enslavement, disenfranchisement, segregation, and discrimination. It is not merely the accidental accretion of neutral state action, applied to a racially divergent social flux. It is an abhorrent expression of who we Americans are as a people, even now, at the dawn of the twenty-first century.

My recitation of the brutal facts about punishment in today's America may sound to some like a primal scream at

this monstrous social machine that is grindir
communities to dust. And I confess that th
times leave me inclined to cry out in despai
ment is intended to be moral, not existential,
thesis is this: we law-abiding, middle-class
made collective decisions on social and in
questions, and we benefit from those dec
benefit from a system of suffering, roote
meted out at our behest. Put differently, o
ety we together have made—first tolera
conditions in our sprawling urban ghet
to act out rituals of punishment again
form of human sacrifice.

It is a central reality of our time
opened up in cognitive skills, the e
stability of family relations, and att
This is the basis, many would hol
prisonment. Yet I maintain that
ment is, as a historical matter, r
social, and cultural factors pecu
tive of its unlovely racial histor
not communal or personal, ach
dividual case we must, of co
There could be no law, and
putation to persons of resp
But the sum of a million c
on its individual merits,
historic wrong. This is, in
the race and social class
punitive policy that we
the state does not on
makes policies in the a
policies are more or l
aggregate policy judg
bility arise.

caught in these structures. Neither are they independent of the behavior of the people who stand outside of them.

Several years ago, I took time to read some of the nonfiction writings of the great nineteenth century Russian novelist Leo Tolstoy. Toward the end of his life he had become an eccentric pacifist and radical Christian social critic. I was stunned at the force of his arguments. What struck me most was Tolstoy's provocative claim that the core of Christianity lies in Jesus' Sermon on the Mount: You see that fellow over there committing some terrible sin? Well, if you have ever lusted, or allowed jealousy, or envy or hatred to enter your own heart, then you are to be equally condemned! This, Tolstoy claims, is the central teaching of the Christian faith: we're all in the same fix.

Now, without invoking any religious authority, I nevertheless want to suggest that there is a grain of truth in this religious sentiment that is relevant to the problem at hand: That is, while the behavioral pathologies and cultural threats that we see in society—the moral erosions "out there"—the crime, drug addiction, sexually transmitted disease, idleness, violence and all manner of deviance—while these are worrisome, nevertheless, our moral crusade against these evils can take on a pathological dimension of its own. We can become self-righteous, legalistic, ungenerous, stiff-necked, and hypocritical. We can fail to see the beam in our own eye. We can neglect to raise questions of social justice. We can blind ourselves to the close relationship that actually exists between, on the one hand, behavioral pathology in the so-called urban underclass of our country and, on the other hand, society-wide factors—like our greed-driven economy, our worship of the self, our endemic culture of materialism, our vacuous political discourses, our declining civic engagement, and our aversion to sacrificing private gain on behalf of much needed social investments. We can fail to see, in other words, that the problems of the so-called underclass—to which we have reacted with a massive, coercive mobilization—are but an expression, at the bottom of the social hierarchy, of a more profound and widespread moral deviance—one involving all of us.

Taking this position does not make me a moral relativist. I merely hold that, when thinking about the lives of the disadvantaged in our society, the fundamental premise that should guide us is that we are all in this together. *Those* people languishing in the corners of our society are *our* people—they are *us*—whatever may be their race, creed, or country of origin, whether they be the crack-addicted, the HIV-infected, the mentally ill homeless, the juvenile drug sellers, or worse. Whatever the malady, and whatever the offense, we're all in the same fix. We're all in this thing together.

Just look at what we have wrought. We Americans have established what, to many an outside observer, looks like a system of racial caste in the center of our great cities. I refer here to millions of stigmatized, feared, and invisible people. The extent of disparity in the opportunity to achieve their full human potential, as between the children of the middle class and the children of the disadvantaged—a disparity that one takes for granted in America—is virtually unrivaled elsewhere in the industrial, advanced, civilized, free world.

Inclusion, Not Exclusion

Yet too many Americans have concluded, in effect, that those languishing at the margins of our society are simply reaping what they have sown. Their suffering is seen as having nothing to do with us—as not being evidence of systemic failures that can be corrected through collective action. Thus, as I noted, we have given up on the ideal of rehabilitating criminals, and have settled for simply warehousing them. Thus we accept—despite much rhetoric to the contrary—that it is virtually impossible effectively to educate the children of the poor. Despite the best efforts of good people and progressive institutions—despite the encouraging signs of moral engagement with these issues that I have seen in my students over the years, and that give me hope—despite these things, it remains the case that, speaking of the country as a whole, there is no broadly based demand for reform, no sense of moral outrage, no anguished self-criticism, no public reflection in the face of this massive, collective failure.

The core of the problem is that the socially marginal are not seen as belonging to the same general public body as the rest of us. It therefore becomes impossible to do just about anything with them. At least implicitly, our political community acts as though some are different from the rest and, because of their culture—because of their bad values, their self-destructive behavior, their malfeasance, their criminality, their lack of responsibility, their unwillingness to engage in hard work—they *deserve* their fate.

But this is quite wrongheaded. What we Americans fail to recognize—not merely as individuals, I stress, but as a political community—is that these ghetto enclaves and marginal spaces of our cities, which are the source of most prison inmates, are products of our own making: Precisely because we do not want those people near us, we have structured the space in our urban environment so as to keep *them* away from *us*. Then, when they fester in their isolation and their marginality, we hypocritically point a finger, saying in effect: "Look at those people. They threaten the civilized body. They must therefore be expelled, imprisoned, controlled." It is not *we* who must take social responsibility to reform our institutions but, rather, it is *they* who need to take personal responsibility for their wrongful acts. It is not we who must set our *collective* affairs aright, but they who must get their *individual* acts together. This posture, I suggest, is inconsistent with the attainment of a just distribution of benefits and burdens in society.

Civic inclusion has been the historical imperative in Western political life for 150 years. And yet—despite our self-declared status as a light unto the nations, as a beacon of hope to freedom-loving peoples everywhere—despite these lofty proclamations, which were belied by images from the rooftops in flooded New Orleans in September 2005,[1] and are contradicted by our overcrowded prisons—the fact is that this historical project of civic inclusion is woefully incomplete in these United States.

At every step of the way, reactionary political forces have declared the futility of pursuing civic inclusion. Yet, in every instance, these forces have been proven wrong. At one time or another, they have derided the inclusion of women, landless peasants, former serfs and slaves, or immigrants more fully in the civic body. Extending to them the franchise, educating their children, providing health and social welfare to them has always been controversial. But this has been the direction in which the self-declared "civilized" and wealthy nations have been steadily moving. . . . This is why we have a progressive federal income tax and an estate tax in this country, why we feed, clothe and house the needy, why we (used to) worry about investing in our cities' infrastructure, and in the human capital of our people. What the brutal facts about punishment in today's America show is that *this American project of civic inclusion remains incomplete.* Nowhere is that incompleteness more evident than in the prisons and jails of America. And this as yet unfulfilled promise of American democracy reveals a yawning chasm between an ugly and uniquely American reality, and our nation's exalted image of herself.

1. New Orleans was devastated by Hurricane Katrina in 2005. Some link the slow response of the federal government to the fact that many of the affected communities were poor African Americans.

Viewpoint 2

> *"The evidence is clear: black prison rates result from crime, not racism."*

America's Imprisonment Practices Are Not Racist

Heather Mac Donald

Heather Mac Donald is a contributing editor of City Journal *and the John M. Olin Fellow at the Manhattan Institute. In the following viewpoint, she maintains that blacks are disproportionately imprisoned because they commit disproportionate amounts of crime. Common arguments which blame black incarceration rates on drug policies or unfair sentencing for crack cocaine use are not born out by statistics or history, Mac Donald insists. Instead, she argues that high rates of imprisonment have been essential in stabilizing inner-city neighborhoods and in helping make poor African American communities safer.*

As you read, consider the following questions:

1. According to Mac Donald, between 1976 and 2005 what percentage of all murders in America were committed by blacks?
2. As the author reports, in 2006, what percentage of federal crack cocaine defendants were black?

Heather Mac Donald, "Is the Criminal-Justice System Racist?" *City Journal*, Spring 2008. Reproduced by permission.

3. According to Mac Donald, what percentage of the increase in state prisoners between 1980 and 1990 came from violent offenders, and what percentage came from drug offenders?

The race industry and its elite enablers take it as self-evident that high black incarceration rates result from discrimination. At a presidential primary debate this Martin Luther King Day [2008], for instance, Senator Barack Obama charged that blacks and whites "are arrested at very different rates, are convicted at very different rates, [and] receive very different sentences . . . for the same crime." Not to be outdone, Senator Hillary Clinton promptly denounced the "disgrace of a criminal-justice system that incarcerates so many more African-Americans proportionately than whites."

Black Crime

If a listener didn't know anything about crime, such charges of disparate treatment might seem plausible. After all, in 2006, blacks were 37.5 percent of all state and federal prisoners, though they're under 13 percent of the national population. About one in 33 black men was in prison in 2006, compared with one in 205 white men and one in 79 Hispanic men. Eleven percent of all black males between the ages of 20 and 34 are in prison or jail. The dramatic rise in the prison and jail population over the last three decades—to 2.3 million people at the end of 2007—has only amplified the racial accusations against the criminal-justice system.

The favorite culprits for high black prison rates include a biased legal system, draconian drug enforcement, and even prison itself. None of these explanations stands up to scrutiny. The black incarceration rate is overwhelmingly a function of black crime. Insisting otherwise only worsens black alienation and further defers a real solution to the black crime problem.

Racial activists usually remain assiduously silent about that problem. But in 2005, the black homicide rate was over seven times higher than that of whites and Hispanics combined, according to the federal Bureau of Justice Statistics. From 1976 to 2005, blacks committed over 52 percent of all murders in America. In 2006, the black arrest rate for most crimes was two to nearly three times blacks' representation in the population. Blacks constituted 39.3 percent of all violent-crime arrests, including 56.3 percent of all robbery and 34.5 percent of all aggravated-assault arrests, and 29.4 percent of all property-crime arrests.

The advocates acknowledge such crime data only indirectly: by charging bias on the part of the system's decision makers. As Obama suggested in the Martin Luther King [Day] debate, police, prosecutors, and judges treat blacks and whites differently "for the same crime."

Law Enforcement Not Race-Based

Let's start with the idea that cops over-arrest blacks and ignore white criminals. In fact, the race of criminals reported by crime victims matches arrest data. As long ago as 1978, a study of robbery and aggravated assault in eight cities found parity between the race of assailants in victim identifications and in arrests—a finding replicated many times since, across a range of crimes. No one has ever come up with a plausible argument as to why crime victims would be biased in their reports.

Moving up the enforcement chain, the campaign against the criminal-justice system next claims that prosecutors overcharge and judges oversentence blacks. Obama describes this alleged postarrest treatment as "Scooter Libby justice for some and Jena justice for others." Jena, Louisiana, of course, was where a D.A. [district attorney] initially lodged attempted second-degree murder charges against black students who, in December 2006, slammed a white student's head against a concrete beam, knocking him unconscious, and then stomped and kicked him in the head while he was down. As Charlotte

Allen has brilliantly chronicled in *The Weekly Standard*, a local civil rights activist crafted a narrative linking the attack to an unrelated incident months earlier, in which three white students hung two nooses from a schoolyard tree—a display that may or may not have been intended as a racial provocation. This entrepreneur then embellished the tale with other alleged instances of redneck racism—above all, the initial attempted-murder charges. An enthusiastic national press responded to the bait exactly as intended, transforming the "Jena Six" into victims rather than perpetrators. In the seven months of ensuing headlines and protests, Jena became a symbol of systemic racial unfairness in America's court system. If blacks were disproportionately in prison, the refrain went, it was because they faced biased prosecutors—like the one in Jena—as well as biased juries and judges.

Backing up this bias claim has been the holy grail of criminology for decades—and the prize remains as elusive as ever. In 1997, criminologists Robert Sampson and Janet Lauritsen reviewed the massive literature on charging and sentencing. They concluded that "large racial differences in criminal offending," not racism, explained why more blacks were in prison proportionately than whites and for longer terms. A 1987 analysis of Georgia felony convictions, for example, found that blacks frequently received disproportionately lenient punishment. A 1990 study of 11,000 California cases found that slight racial disparities in sentence length resulted from blacks' prior records and other legally relevant variables. A 1994 Justice Department survey of felony cases from the country's 75 largest urban areas discovered that blacks actually had a lower chance of prosecution following a felony than whites did and that they were less likely to be found guilty at trial. Following conviction, blacks were more likely to receive prison sentences, however—an outcome that reflected the gravity of their offenses as well as their criminal records. . . .

This consensus hasn't made the slightest dent in the ongoing search for systemic racism. An entire industry in the law schools now dedicates itself to flushing out prosecutorial and judicial bias, using ever more complicated statistical artillery. The net result? A few new studies show tiny, unexplained racial disparities in sentencing, while other analyses continue to find none. Any differences that do show up are trivially small compared with the exponentially greater rates of criminal offending among blacks. No criminologist would claim, moreover, to have controlled for every legal factor that affects criminal-justice outcomes, says Patrick Langan, former senior statistician for the Bureau of Justice Statistics. Prosecutors and judges observe the heinousness of a defendant's conduct, for example, but a number-crunching researcher has no easy way to discover and quantify that variable.

Some criminologists replace statistics with High Theory in their search for racism. The criminal-justice system does treat individual suspects and criminals equally, they concede. But the problem is how society *defines* crime and criminals. Crime is a social construction designed to marginalize minorities, these theorists argue. A liberal use of scare quotes is virtually mandatory in such discussions, to signal one's distance from primitive notions like "law-abiding" and "dangerous." Arguably, vice crimes are partly definitional (though even there, the law enforcement system focuses on them to the extent that they harm communities). But the social constructivists are talking about all crime, and it's hard to see how one could "socially reconstruct" assault or robbery so as to convince victims that they haven't been injured.

Drug Policies Not to Blame

Unfair drug policies are an equally popular explanation for black incarceration rates. Legions of pundits, activists, and academics charge that the war on drugs is a war on minorities—a de facto war at best, an intentional one at worst.

Playing a starring role in this conceit are federal crack penalties, the source of the greatest amount of misinformation in the race and incarceration debate. Crack is a smokeable and highly addictive cocaine concentrate, created by cooking powder cocaine until it hardens into pellets called "rocks." Crack produces a faster—and more potent—high than powder cocaine, and it's easier to use, since smoking avoids the unpleasantness of needles and is more efficient than snorting. Under the 1986 federal Anti-Drug Abuse Act, getting caught with five grams of crack carries a mandatory minimum five-year sentence in federal court; to trigger the same five-year minimum, powder-cocaine traffickers would have to get caught with 500 grams. On average, federal crack sentences are three to six times longer than powder sentences for equivalent amounts.

The media love to target the federal crack penalties because crack defendants are likely to be black. In 2006, 81 percent of federal crack defendants were black, while only 27 percent of federal powder-cocaine defendants were. Since federal crack rules are more severe than those for powder, and crack offenders are disproportionately black, those rules must explain why so many blacks are in prison, the conventional wisdom holds.

But consider the actual number of crack sellers sentenced in federal court each year. In 2006, 5,619 were tried federally, 4,495 of them black. From 1996 to 2000, the federal courts sentenced more powder traffickers (23,743) than crack traffickers (23,121). It's going to take a lot more than 5,000 or so crack defendants a year to account for the 562,000 black prisoners in state and federal facilities at the end of 2006—or the 858,000 black prisoners in custody overall, if one includes the population of county and city jails. Nor do crack/powder disparities at the state level explain black incarceration rates: only 13 states distinguish between crack and powder sentences, and they employ much smaller sentence differentials. . . .

Crack Epidemic Was Real

Nevertheless, the federal crack penalties dominate discussions on race and incarceration because they seem to provide a concrete example of egregious racial disparity. This leads to a commonly expressed syllogism: crack penalties have a disparate impact on blacks; disparate impact is racist; therefore, crack penalties are racist. This syllogism has been particularly prominent recently, thanks to the U.S. Sentencing Commission's 2007 decision to lighten federal crack penalties retroactively in the name of racial equity.

The press has covered this development voraciously, serving up a massive dose of crack revisionism aimed at proving the racist origins of the war on crack. Crack was never a big deal, the revisionist story line goes. But when Boston Celtics draft pick Len Bias died of a crack overdose in 1986, the media went into overdrive covering the crack phenomenon. "Images—or perhaps anecdotes—about the evils of crack, and the street crime it was presumed to stoke" circulated, as the *New York Times* archly put it in a December 2007 article. A "moral panic" ensued about an imaginary threat from a powerless minority group. Whites feared that addicted blacks would invade their neighborhoods. Sensational stories about "crack babies" surfaced. All this hysteria resulted in the unnecessary federal crack penalties.

Since the 1980s, the revisionist narrative continues, experts have determined that powder and crack show more pharmacological "similarities than differences," in the *Times*'s words, and that crack is no more damaging to fetuses than alcohol. The belief that crack was an inner-city scourge was thus a racist illusion, and the sentencing structure to quell it a racist assault. Or, as U.S. District Judge Clyde Cahill put it, in what one hopes is not a representative sample of the federal judicial temperament: "Legislators' unconscious racial aversion towards blacks, sparked by unsubstantiated reports of the effects of crack, reactionary media prodding, and an agitated constituency, motivated the legislators . . . to produce a dual system of punishment."

Leave aside the irony of the press's now declaring smugly that the press exaggerated the ravages of crack. (The same *New York Times* that now sneers at "images—or perhaps anecdotes—about the evils of crack" ran searing photos of crack addicts in 1993 that included a woman kneeling before a crack dealer, unzipping his fly, a baby clinging to her back; such degraded prostitutes, known as "strawberries," were pervasive casualties of the epidemic.) The biggest problem with the revisionist narrative is its unreality. The assertion that concern about crack resulted from "unconscious racial aversion towards blacks" ignores a key fact: black leaders were the first to sound the alarm about the drug, as Harvard law professor Randall Kennedy documents in *Race, Crime, and the Law*. Harlem congressman Charles Rangel initiated the federal response to the epidemic, warning the House of Representatives in March 1986 that crack had made cocaine "frightening[ly]" accessible to youth. A few months later, Brooklyn congressman Major Owens explicitly rejected what is now received wisdom about media hype. "None of the press accounts really have exaggerated what is actually going on," Owens said; the crack epidemic was "as bad as any articles have stated." Queens congressman Alton Waldon then called on his colleagues to act: "For those of us who are black this self-inflicted pain is the worst oppression we have known since slavery. . . . Let us . . . pledge to crack down on crack." The bill that eventually passed, containing the crack/powder distinction, won majority support among black congressmen, none of whom, as Kennedy points out, objected to it as racist.

A Logical Sentencing Scheme

These politicians were reacting to a devastating outbreak of inner-city violence and addiction unleashed by the new form of cocaine. Because crack came in small, easily digestible amounts, it democratized what had been a rarefied drug, making an intense high available to people with very little money. The crack market differed radically from the discreet phone transactions and private deliveries that characterized powder-cocaine distribution: volatile young dealers sold crack on street corners, using guns to establish their turf. Crack, homicides, and assaults went hand in hand; certain areas of New York became "like a war zone," retired DEA [Drug Enforcement Administration] special agent Robert Stutman told PBS's [Public Broadcasting Service's] *Frontline* in 2000. The large national spike in violence in the mid-1980s was largely due to the crack trade, and its victims were overwhelmingly black inner-city residents. . . .

It takes shameless sleight of hand to turn an effort to protect blacks into a conspiracy against them. If Congress had ignored black legislators' calls to increase cocaine-trafficking penalties, the outcry among the groups now crying racism would have been deafening. Yes, a legislative bidding war drove federal crack penalties ultimately to an arbitrary and excessive point; the reduction of those penalties is appropriate. But what led to the crack-sentencing scheme wasn't racism but legal logic. Prosecutors rely on heavy statutory penalties to induce defendants to spill the beans on their criminal colleagues. "An amazing public spirit is engendered when you tell someone he is facing 150 years to life but has the possibility of getting out after eight if he tells you who committed a string of homicides," says Walter Arsenault, who headed the Manhattan district attorney's homicide-investigation unit in the 1980s and 1990s. . . .

Untrue Claims

Critics follow up their charges about crack with several empirical claims about drugs and imprisonment. None is true. The first is that drug enforcement has been the most important cause of the overall rising incarceration rate since the

Homicide Offending Rates per 100,000 Population by Race, 1985–2005

	White	Black	Other
1985	5.1	34.0	5.8
1986	5.3	37.9	6.0
1987	5.2	36.6	5.0
1988	4.9	41.2	4.5
1989	5.1	42.0	4.7
1990	5.6	46.6	4.2
1991	5.6	51.4	5.4
1992	5.2	47.0	5.7
1993	5.2	49.2	5.6
1994	5.1	45.4	5.1
1995	4.9	39.3	5.4
1996	4.5	35.9	4.8
1997	4.1	32.2	4.5
1998	4.2	27.8	3.9
1999	3.6	25.4	3.9
2000	3.5	25.6	3.3
2001	3.5	25.6	3.0
2002	3.6	25.0	2.9
2003	3.5	25.3	3.4
2004	3.6	24.1	2.7
2005	3.5	26.5	2.8

TAKEN FROM: "Homicide Trends in the U.S.," Office of Justice Web Site, July 11, 2007. www.ojp.usdoj.gov.

1980s. Yet even during the most rapid period of population growth in prisons—from 1980 to 1990—36 percent of the growth in state prisons (where 88 percent of the nation's prisoners are housed) came from violent crimes, compared with 33 percent from drug crimes. Since then, drug offenders have played an even smaller role in state prison expansion. From 1990 to 2000, violent offenders accounted for 53 percent of the census increase—and all of the increase from 1999 to 2004.

Next, critics blame drug enforcement for rising racial disparities in prison. Again, the facts say otherwise. In 2006, blacks were 37.5 percent of the 1,274,600 state prisoners. If you remove drug prisoners from that population, the percentage of black prisoners drops to 37 percent—half of a percentage point, hardly a significant difference. (No criminologist, to the best of my knowledge, has ever performed this exercise.)

The rise of drug cases in the criminal-justice system has been dramatic, it's important to acknowledge. In 1979, drug offenders were 6.4 percent of the state prison population; in 2004, they were 20 percent. Even so, violent and property offenders continue to dominate the ranks: in 2004, 52 percent of state prisoners were serving time for violence and 21 percent for property crimes, for a combined total over three and a half times that of state drug offenders. In federal prisons, drug offenders went from 25 percent of all federal inmates in 1980 to 47.6 percent of all federal inmates in 2006. Drug-war opponents focus almost exclusively on federal, as opposed to state, prisons because the proportion of drug offenders is highest there. But the federal system held just 12.3 percent of the nation's prisoners in 2006.

Prison Does Not Cause Crime

So much for the claim that blacks are disproportionately imprisoned because of the war on drugs. But a final, even more audacious, argument maintains that incarceration itself, not criminals, causes crime in black neighborhoods. Because blacks have the highest prison rate, this argument holds, incarceration constitutes an unjust and disproportionate burden on them. This idea has gained wide currency in the academic world and in anti-incarceration think tanks. Columbia University law professor Jeffrey Fagan offered a representative version of the theory in a 2003 law review article co-authored with two public health researchers. Sending black males to prison "weakens the general social control of children and especially adolescents," Fagan writes. Incarceration increases the number of single-parent households. With adult males missing from their neighborhoods, boys will be more likely to get involved in crime, since they lack proper supervision. The net result: "Incarceration begets more incarceration [in] a vicious cycle."

A few questions present themselves. How many convicts were living in a stable relationship with the mother (or one of the mothers) of their children before being sent upstate? (Forget even asking about their marriage rate.) What kind of positive guidance do men who are committing enough crimes to end up in prison, rather than on probation (an exceedingly high threshold), provide to young people? Further, if Fagan is right that keeping criminals out of prison and on the streets preserves a community's social capital, inner cities should have thrived during the 1960s and early 1970s, when prison resources contracted sharply. In fact, New York's poorest neighborhoods—the subject of Fagan's analysis—turned around only in the 1990s, when the prison population reached its zenith.

Fagan, like many other criminologists, conflates the effects of prison and crime. Neighborhoods with high incarceration rates suffer disproportionate burdens, he claims. Firms are reluctant to locate in such areas, decreasing job opportunities. Police pay closer attention to these high-incarceration zones, increasing the chance that any given criminal within them will wind up arrested. Thus, incarceration "provides a steady supply of offenders for more incarceration." But if business owners think twice about certain communities, it's because they fear crime, not a high concentration of ex-convicts per se. It's unlikely that prospective employers even know the population of ex-cons in a neighborhood; what they are aware of is its crime rates. And an employer who hesitates to hire an ex-con is almost certainly reacting to his criminal record, even if he has been given community probation instead of prison. Likewise, if the police give extra scrutiny to neighborhoods with many ex-convicts, it's because those convicts commit a lot of crime. Finally, putting more criminals on probation, rather than sending them to prison—as Fagan and others advocate—would only increase law enforcement surveillance of high-crime neighborhoods.

This popular "social ecological" analysis of incarceration, as Fagan and other criminologists call it, treats prison like an outbreak of infectious disease that takes over certain communities, felling people on a seemingly random basis. "As the risks of going to jail or prison grow over time for persons living in those areas, their prospects for marriage or earning a living and family-sustaining wage diminish as the incarceration rates around them rise," Fagan says. This analysis elides [cuts out] the role of individual will. Fagan and others assume that once one lives in a high-incarceration—that is, high-crime—area, one can do little to avoid prison. But even in the most frayed urban communities, plenty of people choose to avoid the "Life." Far from facing diminished marriage prospects, an upstanding, reliable young man in the inner city would be regarded as a valuable catch.

No one doubts that having a criminal record—whether it results in community probation or prison—is a serious handicap. People convicted of crimes compete for jobs at a clear disadvantage with those who have stayed crime-free. But for all the popularity of the view that the system is to blame, it's not hard to find dissenters who believe that individuals are responsible for the decision to break the law. "My position is not hard," says public housing manager Matthew Kennedy. "You don't have to do that crime." Kennedy supported President Bill Clinton's controversial 1996 "one-strike" rule for public housing, which allowed housing authorities to evict drug dealers and other lawbreaking tenants on their first offense. "I'm trying to protect the good people in my community," Kennedy explains. "A criminal record is preventable. It's all on you." Kennedy has no truck with the argument that it is unfair to send ex-offenders back to prison for violations of their parole conditions, such as staying away from their gang associates and hangouts. "Where do they take responsibility for their own actions?" he wonders. "You've been told, 'Don't come back to this community.' Why would you come back here? You've got to change your ways, change the habits that got you in there in the first place."

Prisons Create Stability

Though you'd never know it from reading the academic literature, some people in minority communities even see prison as potentially positive for individuals as well as for communities. "I don't buy the idea that there's no sense to prison," says Clyde Fulford, a 54-year-old lifelong resident of the William Mead Homes, a downtown Los Angeles housing project. Having raised his children to be hardworking, law-abiding citizens, Fulford is a real role model for his neighborhood, not the specious drug-dealing kind posited by the "social ecological" theory of incarceration. "I know a lot of people who went to prison," Fulford says. "A lot changed they life for the better. Prison was they wake-up call." Is prison unavoidable and thus unfair? "They knew they was going to pay. It's up to that person." What if the prisoners hadn't been locked up? "Many would be six feet under."

Robert Grace, the Los Angeles prosecutor, is acutely aware of the fragility and preciousness of the rule of law. "As a civilized society, we can't allow what's happening in Latin America to take over here," he says. "Venezuela and Mexico are awash in appalling violence because they don't respect the law." Thus, when prominent figures like Barack Obama make sweeping claims about racial unfairness in the criminal-justice system, they play with fire. "For any political candidate to make such claims out of expediency is wrong," Grace says. "If they have statistics that back up the claim, I'd like to see them. But to create phony perceptions of injustice is as wrong as not doing anything about the real thing."

The evidence is clear: black prison rates result from crime, not racism. America's comparatively high rates of incarceration are nothing to celebrate, of course, but the alternative is far worse. The dramatic drop in crime in the 1990s, to which stricter sentencing policies unquestionably contributed, has freed thousands of law-abiding inner-city residents from the bondage of fear. Commerce and street life have revived in those urban neighborhoods where crime has fallen most.

The pressure to divert even more offenders from prison, however, will undoubtedly grow. If a probation system can finally be crafted that provides as much public safety as prison, we should welcome it. But the continuing search for the chimera of criminal-justice bigotry is a useless distraction that diverts energy and attention from the crucial imperative of helping more inner-city boys stay in school—and out of trouble.

Viewpoint 3

> *"In drug cases, where the ultimate goal is to rid society of the entire trafficking enterprise, mandatory minimum statutes are especially significant."*

Mandatory Minimum Sentencing Is Just in Drug Cases

Jodi L. Avergun

Jodi L. Avergun served as chief of staff to the head of the Drug Enforcement Administration (DEA) from 2005 to 2006. In the following viewpoint, she maintains that certain kinds of heinous crimes involving drugs and children must be prosecuted forcefully. She argues that mandatory minimum sentences help deter criminals and are an important and just prosecutorial tool in drug cases, where the threat of long sentences encourages criminals to cooperate with law enforcement and implicate other perpetrators.

Jodi L. Avergun, "Testimony Before the House Judiciary Committee Subcommittee on Crime, Terrorism and Homeland Security," *Defending America's Most Vulnerable: Safe Access to Drug Treatment and Child Protection Act of 2005—H.R. 1528*, April 12, 2005, pp. 7–9. http://www.access.gpo.gov/congress/house/pdf/109hrg/20527.pdf.

As you read, consider the following questions:

1. According to Avergun, how many children were affected in clandestine meth lab–related incidents between 2000 and the beginning of 2005?
2. According to the author, the Department of Justice has no specific weapons against those who distribute controlled substances within the vicinity of what kind of facility?
3. Mandatory minimum sentences are especially appropriate in what two kinds of trafficking, according to Avergun?

The DEA [Drug Enforcement Administration] has seen firsthand the devastation that illegal drugs cause in the lives of children. Children are our nation's future and our most precious resource, and, sadly, many of them are having their lives and dreams stolen by illegal drugs. This theft takes many forms, from a drug addicted parent who neglects a child, to a clandestine methamphetamine "cook" using a child's play area as a laboratory site, to a parent using a child to serve as camouflage for their "stash," to a child being present during a drug transaction. The list goes on and on, but the end result remains the same: innocent children needlessly suffer from being exposed to illegal drugs.

The PROTECT Act

The Department of Justice and other law enforcement agencies at all levels seek to protect the most vulnerable segments of our society from those drug traffickers and drug addicted individuals who exploit those individuals least able to protect themselves. In 2003, Congress made significant strides in this area by enacting the Prosecutorial Remedies and Other Tools to end the Exploitation of Children Today Act, better known as the PROTECT Act. This law has proven effective in enabling law enforcement to pursue and to punish wrongdoers who threaten the youth of America. Last year [2004, Committee] Chairman [Jim] Sensenbrenner introduced H.R. [House of Representatives] 4547, the "Defending America's Most Vulnerable: Safe Access to Drug Treatment and Child Protection Act of 2004," which would have taken these efforts even further by focusing on the scourge of drug trafficking in some of its most base and dangerous forms: those who use minors to commit trafficking offenses, trafficking to minors, trafficking in places where minors are present, and trafficking in or near drug treatment centers. . . . We . . . reiterate our support for legislation that addresses drug-related incidents involving minors.

The endangerment of children through exposure to drug activity, sales of drugs to children, the use of minors in drug trafficking, and the peddling of pharmaceutical and other illicit drugs to drug treatment patients are all significant problems today. Sadly, the horrific examples below are just a few instances where children have been found victimized and exploited by people whose lives have been taken over by drugs:

- From . . . 2000 through the first quarter of . . . 2005, over 15,000 children were reported as being affected in clandestine [methamphetamine] laboratory-related incidents.[1] The term "affected children" is defined as a child being present and/or evidence that a child lived at a clandestine laboratory site. This total reflects only those instances where law enforcement was involved. The true number of children affected by clandestine laboratory incidents is unknown, though it is surely much greater.

1. Methamphetamine is a very potent stimulant drug which can be synthesized in home laboratories.

- In 2004, a defendant from Iowa pled guilty to conspiring to manufacture methamphetamine. Although the meth was not manufactured in the defendant's home, where the defendant's 4-year-old son also lived, [it] was used as the distribution point for large quantities of meth. The son's hair tested positive for extremely high levels of meth, indicating chronic exposure to the drug. In this case, no enhancement[2] could be applied because of the son's exposure, as he had not been endangered during the actual manufacture of the meth.
- In November 2004, the DEA raided a suspected methamphetamine lab located in a home in Missouri. During this operation three children, all under five years of age, were found sleeping on chemical-soaked rugs. The residence was filled with insects and rodents and had no electricity or running water. Two guard dogs kept by the "cooks" to fend off law enforcement were also found: clean, healthy, and well-fed. The dogs actually ate off a dinner plate.

Currently, investigations targeting individuals involved in the manufacture of methamphetamine or amphetamine which are prosecuted on a federal level have a sentencing enhancement available. This enhancement provides . . . about 8 to 10 years for a first offender when a substantial risk of harm to the life of a minor or an incompetent individual is created. Unfortunately, investigations targeting traffickers involved in the distribution of other illegal drugs, such as heroin or cocaine, do not have this same enhancement. . . .

Prosecutions and Minimums

The Department of Justice is committed to vigorously prosecuting drug trafficking in all of its egregious forms. Prosecutions range from high-level international drug traffickers to

2. Certain crimes may carry longer, or enhanced, sentences if the perpetrator endangers children or commits some other defined act.

Mandatory Minimums Are Legal and Popular

Over the past 20 years, Congress has passed tough but fair mandatory minimum sentences for certain particularly dangerous crimes. . . .

These ensure that the worst criminals stay behind bars for meaningful periods of time, keeping them off our streets and away from our families, and making would-be offenders think twice about risking a long prison sentence.

That's why mandatory minimum laws repeatedly have been enacted by Congress . . . and why tough sentencing enjoys widespread public support.

Source: Leonardo M. Rapadas,
"OPED: Mandatory Minimum Sentences Keep Streets Safe,"
Pacific Daily News *(Guam), August 7, 2004.*

street-level predators who are tempting children or addicts with the lure of profit and the promise of intoxication.

We have had some successes. Statistics maintained by the U.S. Sentencing Commission indicate that between 1998 and 2002 over 300 defendants were sentenced annually under the guideline that provides for enhanced penalties for drug activity involving protected locations, minors, or pregnant individuals. But our tools are limited. And we have no specific weapon against those who distribute controlled substances within the vicinity of a drug treatment center.

The people who would sink to the depths of inhumanity by targeting their trafficking activity at those with the least ability to resist such offers are deserving the most severe punishment. The Department of Justice cannot and will not tolerate this conduct in a free and safe America, and that is why the Department of Justice stands firmly behind the intent of this legislation to increase the punishment meted out to those who would harm us, our children, and those seeking to escape the cycle of addiction.

The Department of Justice supports mandatory minimum sentences in appropriate circumstances. In a way sentencing guidelines cannot, mandatory minimum statutes provide a level of uniformity and predictability in sentencing. They deter certain types of criminal behavior determined by Congress to be sufficiently egregious as to merit harsh penalties by clearly forewarning the potential offender and the public at large of the minimum potential consequences of committing such an offense. And mandatory minimum sentences can also incapacitate dangerous offenders for long periods of time, thereby increasing public safety. Equally important, mandatory minimum sentences provide an indispensable tool for prosecutors, because they provide the strongest incentive to defendants to cooperate against the others who were involved in their criminal activity.

In drug cases, where the ultimate goal is to rid society of the entire trafficking enterprise, mandatory minimum statutes are especially significant. Unlike a bank robbery, for which a bank teller or an ordinary citizen could be a critical witness, often in drug cases the critical witnesses are drug users and/or other drug traffickers. The offer of relief from a mandatory minimum sentence in exchange for truthful testimony allows the Government to move steadily and effectively up the chain of supply, using the lesser distributors to prosecute the more serious dealers and their leaders and suppliers. Mandatory minimum sentences are needed in appropriate circumstances, such as trafficking involving minors and trafficking in and around drug treatment centers.

VIEWPOINT 4

> *"The people bearing the brunt of mandatory sentencing are not the affluent or the middle class."*

Mandatory Minimum Sentencing Is Unjust

Robert Hooker and Robert Hirsh

Robert Hooker was the public defender of Pima County, Arizona, before his death in 2008; Robert Hirsh succeeded him. In this viewpoint, the two authors argue that Arizona's high incarceration and recidivism rates are linked to mandatory minimum sentences. They also maintain that the use of mandatory minimums results in most cases being settled through plea bargaining rather than trial and that this unduly impacts poor defendants who cannot pay for expensive legal representation. Hooker and Hirsh conclude that Arizona should establish a commission to review sentencing and roll back the use of mandatory minimums.

As you read, consider the following questions:

1. According to the authors, what is Arizona's recidivism rate?

Robert Hooker and Robert Hirsh, "Sentencing Laws Are Senseless," *Arizona Daily Star*, March 2, 2008. Reproduced by permission of Robert Hirsh.

2. How many prisoners over age fifty were in custody in Arizona at the time the article was written?
3. According to the authors, what kind of judicial review are plea bargains subject to?

[Arizona] Gov. Janet Napolitano's 2008–2009 proposed budget includes almost $1 billion for the annual expense of maintaining our adult and juvenile prison system. The state is also receiving bids for the construction of facilities to create 3,000 additional prison beds to ease prison overcrowding. The standard construction cost is $110,000 and up per bed.

In the last 10 years the incarceration rate in the United States has far outpaced the rest of the world. We lock up people at five to eight times the rate of any other industrialized country.

Excessive Incarceration

Arizona ranks with Mississippi, Louisiana, and Texas as having one of the highest incarceration rates in the United States, including particularly high rates of incarceration for women and minorities.

A 2007 study projects a 60 percent prison population increase in the next decade. At that rate, the Department of Corrections would have to add 2,000 beds every year to keep up. This means a minimum $40 million yearly budget increase for prison operations, and huge capital outlays to cover the never-ending construction of new facilities.

These sums don't include funding for any rehabilitative programs, because by law Arizona prisoners go to prison to receive their "just deserts," and not for help. Incredibly, Arizona's large numbers of DUI [driving under the influence of alcohol] offenders don't have access to alcohol rehabilitation programs in our prisons. It's little wonder that Arizona's recidivism [reoffense and rearrest] rate remains close to 70 percent.

If these mind-boggling amounts of money were buying us public safety, or even helping to support a more ordered society, they might be acceptable. The facts show otherwise:

- 49 percent of new prison admissions are for parole or probation violations.
- 55 percent of Arizona prisoners are serving time for non-violent offenses—DUI, drugs, theft, etc.
- Only 18 percent are in prison for offenses involving victim injuries. Many are serving time for automobile accidents criminalized by allegations of negligent or reckless behavior, frequently alcohol-related.

At the present time, Arizona has more than 2,000 inmates over 50 years old who will remain in custody well into their geriatric years, and many for life. These prisoners, well beyond their lawbreaking years, require special medical attention, expenses that must be borne by the taxpayers.

Finally, there is no direct relationship between incarceration rates and crime rates. The opposite is true. States with higher rates of incarceration have comparatively lower rates of reduction of crime.

Too Many Mandatory Minimums

High incarceration rates are driven by a tough criminal code that mandates long prison terms for a variety of offenses, violent or not. The only accused persons in Arizona who are not facing mandatory minimums are first-time defendants accused of small-dollar-amount property crimes, or offenses involving small quantities of drugs.

In other cases, a felony conviction generally, by law, means a term of mandatory incarceration. An accused faces manda-

Overcrowding in Arizona Prisons

[Reporter] Jeffrey Brown: [Director of the Arizona Department of Corrections Dora] Schriro, who arrived in Arizona . . . from the top prisons job in Missouri, is fighting an uphill battle against overcrowding. The state's prison population has skyrocketed, up 50 percent between 1995 and 2005 and growing.

And a big part of the problem is repeat offenders. A recent study showed that nearly half of Arizona's inmates return to prison within three years of being released.

Representative Bill Konopnicki: If we don't make some changes, we're going to need to invest about $3 billion in just hardcore facilities to house these prisoners. And then 97 percent of them at some point are released, and we have had very few programs that actually let them reenter [society] successfully.

And so that's the perfect storm, the shortage on budget, shortage on beds, increased population, increased prison population, and no way to make that transition.

Online NewsHour, *July 22, 2008. www.pbs.org.*

tory sentencing if he has any past felony conviction, or if he is accused of being a repetitive offender. As to the former, any past conviction counts, no matter how old. As to the latter, one would become a repetitive offender if he were to sell a marijuana cigarette on one day, and repeat that act the next day. All these trigger mandatory sentences at conviction.

Because of this, Arizona's criminal-justice system operates through plea bargains rather than trials. Statewide, less than 5 percent of all criminal cases are disposed of by trial. Prosecutors rather than judges make the sentencing determinations.

These decisions are not subject to judicial review and are made behind closed doors. They are not made in conformity with any standard judicial safeguards. There is no input from probation officers or even information from the accused or their families.

In Pima County, prosecutors refuse plea bargains in cases involving repetitive drug sales. In the past, they refused pleas in felony DUI cases.

Prosecutors' plea policies vary from county to county, depending on the political winds of the day. A past survey showed more than 50 public-defender clients sentenced to over eight years in prison for drunken driving convictions, and one person had been sentenced to a combined total of 20 years for two separate DUI crimes. These prosecutions, however harsh and senseless, were politically supported because of an all-out war against drunken driving.

Many cases are troubling: Community supervision would permit non-dangerous offenders to maintain their employment and support their families. Arizona's mandatory sentencing often makes that impossible.

The people bearing the brunt of mandatory sentencing are not the affluent or the middle class. A recent survey revealed that the plea bargains offered to accused persons hiring private attorneys are markedly better than those offered to attorneys appointed for indigent defendants.

The result is that we incarcerate large numbers of our poor for substantial periods of time. These people, separated from their families, then go on the treadmill of intergenerational poverty and prison.

There is a solution. Despite the fact that few politicians ever espouse legislation perceived to be "soft on crime," many see that our mandatory-sentencing laws are needlessly expensive and ineffective in decreasing crime.

In recent years other states have set up commissions to review their justice systems. These reviews have resulted in cutting back mandatory sentences without a consequent diminution of public safety.

It's time the public and the politicians get the facts on how expensive and unfair our criminal-justice system is and submit all of it to the light of public examination.

VIEWPOINT 5

"It is the totally inhumane and callous policy of the swift release of drug addicts from prison that is harmful to them, not their imprisonment in the first place."

Imprisoning Drug Users Is Just

Theodore Dalrymple

Theodore Dalrymple is the pen name of British writer and retired prison and inner city doctor and psychiatrist Anthony Daniels. In the following viewpoint, he argues that imprisoning drug addicts benefits them by preventing them from getting drugs. He also argues that treatment is not a good alternative to prison, because criminality is not caused by addiction, and therefore treating addiction will not prevent crime. Dalrymple concludes that it is the poor who are most harmed when drug addicts are released from prison.

As you read, consider the following questions:

1. How much time does Dalrymple suggest that drug use should add onto the sentence for any crime committed?

Theodore Dalrymple, "It Is Right to Imprison Drug Addicts," Social Affairs Unit, March 18, 2008. Reproduced by permission.

2. According to the author, is addiction a bona fide medical condition?

3. According to Dalrymple, if drug addicts truly cannot help themselves, should they be given shorter sentences or longer sentences?

An item in this week's [March 18, 2008,] *Observer* [a liberal British newspaper] caught my eye. It was a report that the UK [United Kingdom] Drug Policy Commission had concluded that, "convicted drug users should not be sent to prison because it does more harm than good."

But to whom or to what does it do more harm to send them to prison? The way the *Observer* puts it, one is reminded of the lady in [Charles] Dickens who thinks there is a pain in the room but cannot positively assert that she has it. Just as a pain cannot exist without a subject to feel it, so a harm must be done to someone or to something in which someone has an interest. So who is harmed by drug users being sent to prison?

There seem to be two main possibilities here: the first is the prisoners themselves, and second is everyone else in society.

Prison Helps Drug Users

Let us take the possibilities in order. Does going to prison harm drug takers?

Contrary to alarmist reports about the number of prisoners taking drugs, the answer is no; indeed the suggestion is the very reverse of the truth. The condition of heroin addicts is frequently pitiable when they arrive in prison: they are frequently malnourished, covered in sores and possessed with abscesses where they have injected themselves. Within two or three months of imprisonment, they look the picture of health.

Unfortunately, it is truth that they often a few months later are back in the condition in which they arrived the time before. I told many prisoners that they would make excellent extras in a film about concentration camps, and they all knew exactly what I meant. It is also the case that some prisoners, having lost their tolerance to heroin while in prison (a testimony to the fact that the easy availability of heroin in prison is exaggerated), sometimes take a celebratory dose of heroin on their release that kills them, though it would not have killed them before their imprisonment.

In other words, it is the totally inhumane and callous policy of the swift release of drug addicts from prison that is harmful to them, not their imprisonment in the first place. The humane as well as the morally correct thing to do would be to treat drug addiction as an aggravating circumstance of criminal activity and give an automatic sentence of five or ten years in addition to any sentence that the crime committed would ordinarily have attracted.

In any case, the assumption that the imprisonment of drug addicts would have been shown to be wrong if it were the case that imprisonment did them harm is itself mistaken, because it supposes that the primary purpose of prison is therapeutic, a form of medical treatment of those imprisoned. But this is nonsense.

No Harm to Society

What harm can sending drug addicts to prison do to the rest of us when they have committed crimes? In the first place, it costs us money that we would rather spend in some other way, preferably by means of a reduction in our taxation. But it is also argued that imprisoning drug addicts who have committed crimes fails to deal with the cause of their criminal activity, and that if they were treated for their addiction, things would be much better.

This argument relies on two assumptions, both false: first, that drug addicts commit crimes because they are addicts, and

Treatment Does Not Work

The question is why are we told treatment does work? Why are studies cited that "prove" that they do? It all comes down to interpretation of the facts. . . . In fact, these non-scientific proclamations are so common and so ludicrous that the scientific community is now publishing articles ridiculing these reports. I direct your attention to "An Invitation to Debate: How to have a high success rate in treatment: advice for evaluators of alcoholism programs" by William R. Miller and Martha Sanchez-Craig. This article appeared in *Addiction*. The abstract reads as follows:

"Two seasoned alcohol treatment researchers offer tongue-in-cheek advice to novice program evaluators faced with increasing pressure to show high success rates. Based on published examples, they advise: (1) choose only good prognosis cases to evaluate; (2) keep follow-up periods as short as possible; (3) avoid control and comparison groups; (4) choose measures carefully; (5) focus only on alcohol outcomes; (6) use liberal definitions of success; (7) rely on self-reporting; and (8) always declare victory regardless of finding."

While Miller and Sanchez-Craig's humor is not lost to us, the tragic truth they expose is not humorous. Alcoholics and drug addicts are dying everyday because of studies that are published proclaiming treatment works when, in fact, everyone in the treatment industry with any ability to be objective knows that it doesn't.

Gerald Brown,
Saint Jude Retreat House Web site, 2003.
www.soberforever.net.

second that addiction is a bona fide medical condition for which a reliable medical cure exists.

Insofar as a causative connection between drug addiction and criminality exists, it is that criminality inclines to addiction and not the other way round. I think it is probably best to put it like this: that mass criminality and mass addiction such as we have now arise from the same socio-cultural roots. Most heroin addicts who end up in prison have long histories of criminality before they ever took heroin; therefore their addiction is only marginal to their criminality.

Further, if in fact it is the case that no medical "treatment" of addicts, to heroin or to other drugs, works in a reliable fashion (and this is the case), and furthermore it is argued that addicts cannot help their criminal activity because of their addiction, the case for locking up addicts for much longer is greatly strengthened. Failure to lock them up, and thereby to separate them from the rest of society, is to invite them to commit more crimes; therefore the imprisonment of drug addicts who have committed crimes cannot possibly be said to do harm to society, unlike setting them free.

So locking up drug addicts who commit crimes does harm neither to them, nor to the rest of society. Failure to do so does very definite harm, both to them as individuals and to society.

Releasing Addicts Hurts the Poor

But there is something more. The harm that is done to society by failure to lock them up for a suitably long time is unequally distributed among the various classes of society. If there were any justice in the world, it would be the readers of the *Observer* whose houses would be burgled by criminal drug addicts left at liberty by the criminal justice system; but there is not justice in the world.

In fact, it is the relatively poor, the working class, that suffers the brunt of the criminal activity of criminal drug addicts, as the slightest acquaintance with British social reality makes abundantly obvious. (This explains why the *Observer*, in its Olympian way, is able to call burglary "a less serious crime"—without, of course, saying what it would consider a serious crime. Moreover, burglary is far more serious in its effects for the poor than the rich.)

Thus, the idea that drug addicts who commit crimes should not be sent to prison is an absolutely typical example of the cruel, heartless, and unimaginative indifference of the educated and intellectual middle classes of Britain to the fate of their less fortunate fellow-citizens of the working class. The only possible benefit of not imprisoning such addicts is that it saves the middle class a little tax to pay for the protection of their poorer fellow-citizens: and even that is very doubtful in the long run. But it is easy to be lenient at other people's expense, and call it generosity of mind.

VIEWPOINT 6

> "We have deprived hundreds of thousands of [drug users] of basic liberties and subjected them to severe hardship conditions, for no good reason."

Imprisoning Nonviolent Drug Users Is Unjust

Michael Huemer

Michael Huemer is a professor of philosophy at the University of Colorado, Boulder. In the following viewpoint, he argues that drug use does not in itself cause harm to others. In addition, he maintains that individuals have the right to do what they will with their bodies within limits, and that drug use falls within those limits. He concludes that imprisoning drug users is a massive injustice, comparable in some ways to the injustice of slavery.

As you read, consider the following questions:

1. According to Huemer, if the drug laws are unjust, how many people are unjustly imprisoned at any given time?
2. The author says he agrees with prohibitionists that people should not be permitted to do what while using drugs?

Michael Huemer, *The New Prohibition*. Lonedell, MO: Accurate Press, 2004. Reproduced by permission.

3. According to Huemer, what important individuals have admitted to using illegal drugs?

Some argue that drug use must be outlawed because drug use harms the user's family, friends, and coworkers, and/or society in general. A report produced by the Office of National Drug Control Policy [ONDCP] states:

> Democracies can flourish only when their citizens value their freedom and embrace personal responsibility. Drug use erodes the individual's capacity to pursue both ideals. It diminishes the individual's capacity to operate effectively in many of life's spheres—as a student, a parent, a spouse, an employee—even as a coworker or fellow motorist. And, while some claim it represents an expression of individual autonomy, drug use is in fact inimical to personal freedom, producing a reduced capacity to participate in the life of the community and the promise of America.

Being a Jerk Is Not a Crime

At least one of these alleged harms—dangerous driving—*is* clearly the business of the state. For this reason, I entirely agree that people should be prohibited from driving while under the influence of drugs. But what about the rest of the alleged harms? . . .

Imagine that [a hypothetical citizen] Howard—. . . for reasons having nothing to do with drugs—does not value freedom, nor does he embrace personal responsibility. It is unclear exactly what this means, but, for good measure, let us suppose that Howard embraces a totalitarian political ideology and denies the existence of free will. He constantly blames other people for his problems and tries to avoid making decisions. Howard is a college student with a part-time job. However, he is a terrible student and worker. He hardly ever studies and frequently misses assignments, as a result of which he gets poor grades. . . . Howard comes to work late and takes no pride in his work. Though he does nothing against our current laws, he is an inattentive and inconsiderate spouse and parent. Nor does he make any effort to participate in the life of his community, or the promise of America. He would rather lie around the house, watching television and cursing the rest of the world for his problems. In short, Howard does all the bad things to his family, friends, coworkers, and society that the ONDCP says *may* result from drug use. And most of this is voluntary.

Should Congress pass laws against what Howard is doing? Should the police then arrest him, and the district attorney prosecute him, for being a loser?

Once again, it seems absurd to suppose that we would arrest and jail someone for behaving in these ways, undesirable as they may be. Since drug use only has a *chance* of causing one to behave in each of these ways, it is even more absurd to suppose that we should arrest and jail people for drug use on the grounds that drug use has these potential effects.

A Right to Use Drugs

Philosopher Douglas Husak has characterized drug prohibition as the greatest injustice perpetrated in the United States since slavery. This is no hyperbole. If the drug laws are unjust, then we have 450,000 people unjustly imprisoned at any given time.

Why think the drug laws are *unjust*? Husak's argument invokes a principle with which few could disagree: it is unjust for the state to punish people without having a good reason for doing so. We have seen the failure of the most common proposed rationales for drug prohibition. If nothing better is forthcoming, then we must conclude that prohibitionists have no rational justification for punishing drug users. We have deprived hundreds of thousands of people of basic liberties and subjected them to severe hardship conditions, for no good reason.

This is bad enough. But I want to say something stronger: it is not just that we are punishing people for no good reason. We are punishing people for exercising their natural rights. Individuals have a right to use drugs. This right is neither absolute nor exceptionless; suppose, for example, that there existed a drug which, once ingested, caused a significant proportion of users, without any further free choices on their part, to attack other people without provocation. I would think that stopping the use of this drug would be the business of the government. But no existing drug satisfies this description. Indeed, though I cannot take time to delve into the matter here, I think it is clear that the drug *laws* cause far more crime than drugs themselves do.

The idea of a right to use drugs derives from the idea that individuals own their own bodies. That is, a person has the right to exercise control over his own body—including the right to decide how it should be used, and to exclude others from using it—in a manner similar to the way one may exercise control over one's (other) property. This statement is somewhat vague; nevertheless, we can see the general idea embodied in common sense morality. Indeed, it seems that if there is *anything* one would have rights to, it would be one's own body. This explains why we think others may not physically attack you or kidnap you. It explains why we do not accept the use of unwilling human subjects for medical experiments, even if the experiments are beneficial to society—the rest of society may not decide to use your body for its own purposes without your permission. . . .

The right to control one's body cannot be interpreted as implying a right to use one's body in *every* conceivable way, any more than we have the right to use our property in every conceivable way. Most importantly, we may not use our bodies to harm others in certain ways, just as we may not use our property to harm others. But drug use seems to be a paradigm case of a legitimate exercise of the right to control one's

Legalization Will Benefit Communities and Police

We simply urge the federal government to retreat. Let cities and states (and, while we're at it, other countries) decide their own drug policies. Many would continue prohibition, but some would try something new. California and its medical marijuana dispensaries provide a good working example, warts and all, that legalized drug distribution does not cause the sky to fall. . . .

Without the drug war, . . . misguided youths wouldn't look up to criminals as role models, our overflowing prisons could hold real criminals, and—most important to us—more police officers wouldn't have to die.

Peter Moskos and Stanford Franklin,
"It's Time to Legalize Drugs," Washington Post,
August 17, 2009. www.washingtonpost.com.

own body. Drug consumption takes place in and immediately around the user's own body; the salient effects occur *inside* the user's body. If we consider drug use merely as altering the user's own body and mind, it is hard to see how anyone who believes in rights at all could deny that it is protected by a right, for: (a) it is hard to see how anyone who believes in rights could deny that individuals have rights over their own bodies and minds, and (b) it is hard to see how anyone who believes in such rights could deny that drug use, considered merely as altering the user's body and mind, is an example of the exercise of one's rights over one's own body and mind.

Prohibitionists Ignore Users' Rights

Consider two ways a prohibitionist might object to this argument. First, a prohibitionist might argue that drug use does not *merely* alter the user's own body and mind, but also harms the user's family, friends, co-workers, and society. I responded to this sort of argument [above]. . . . Not just *any* way in which an action might be said to "harm" other people makes the action worthy of criminal sanctions. Here we need not try to state a general criterion for what sorts of harms make an action worthy of criminalization; it is enough to note that there are some kinds of "harms" that virtually no one would take to warrant criminal sanctions, and that these include the "harms" I cause to others by being a poor student, an incompetent worker, or an apathetic citizen. That said, I agree with the prohibitionists at least this far: no one should be permitted to drive or operate heavy machinery while under the influence of drugs that impair their ability to do those things; nor should pregnant mothers be permitted to ingest drugs, if it can be proven that those drugs cause substantial risks to their babies (I leave aside the issue of what the threshold level of risk should be, as well as the empirical questions concerning the actual level of risk created by illegal drugs—I don't know those things). But, in the great majority of cases, drug use does not harm anyone in any *relevant* ways—that is, ways that we normally take to merit criminal penalties—and should not be outlawed.

Second, a prohibitionist might argue that drug use fails to qualify as an exercise of the user's rights over his own body, because the individual is not truly acting freely in deciding to use drugs. Perhaps individuals only use drugs because they have fallen prey to some sort of psychological compulsion, because drugs exercise a siren-like allure that distorts users' perceptions, because users don't realize how bad drugs are, or something of that sort. The exact form of this objection doesn't matter; in any case, the prohibitionist faces a dilemma. If users do not freely choose to use drugs, then it is unjust to *punish* them for using drugs. For if users do not choose freely, then they are not morally responsible for their decision, and it is unjust to punish a person for something he is not responsible for. But if users *do* choose freely in deciding to use drugs, then this choice is an exercise of their rights over their own bodies.

I have tried to think of the best arguments prohibitionists could give, but in fact prohibitionists have remained puzzlingly silent on this issue. When a country goes to war, it tends to focus on how to win, sparing little thought for the rights of the victims in the enemy country. Similarly, one effect of America's declaring "war" on drug users seems to have been that prohibitionists have given almost no thought to the rights of drug users. . . .

Drug War Morally Indefensible

Undoubtedly, the drug war has been disastrous in many ways that others can more ably describe—in terms of its effects on crime, on police corruption, and on other civil liberties, to name a few. But more than that, the drug war is morally outrageous in its very conception. If we are to retain some sort of respect for human rights, we cannot deploy force to deprive people of their liberty and property for whimsical reasons. The exercise of such coercion requires a powerful and clearly-stated rationale. Most of the reasons that have actually been proposed in the case of drug prohibition would be considered feeble if advanced in other contexts. Few would take seriously the suggestion that people should be imprisoned for harming their own health, being poor students, or failing to share in the American dream. It is still less credible that we should imprison people for an activity that only *may* lead to those consequences. Yet these and other, similarly weak arguments form the core of prohibition's defense.

Prohibitionists are likewise unable to answer the argument that individuals have a right to use drugs. Any such answer would have to deny either that persons have rights of control over their own bodies, or that consuming drugs constituted an exercise of those rights. We have seen that the sort of harms drug use allegedly causes to society do not make a case against its being an exercise of the user's rights over his own body. And the claim that drug users can't control their behavior or don't know what they are doing renders it even more mysterious why one would believe drug users deserve to be punished for what they are doing. . . .

The harm of being unjustly imprisoned is qualitatively comparable (though it usually ends sooner) to the harm of being enslaved. The increasingly popular scapegoating and stereotyping of drug users and sellers on the part of our nation's leaders is comparable to the racial prejudices of previous generations. Yet very few seem willing to speak on behalf of drug users. Perhaps the unwillingness of those in public life to defend drug users' rights stems from the negative image we have of drug users and the fear of being associated with them. Yet these attitudes remain baffling. I have used illegal drugs myself. I know many decent and successful individuals, both in and out of my profession, who have used illegal drugs. One United States President, one Vice-President, a Speaker of the House, and a Supreme Court Justice have all admitted to having used illegal drugs. More than a third of all Americans over the age of 11 have used illegal drugs. But now leave aside the absurdity of recommending criminal sanctions for all these people. My point is this: if we are convinced of the injustice of drug prohibition, then—even if our protests should fall on deaf ears—we can not remain silent in the face of such a large-scale injustice in our own country. And, fortunately, radical social reforms *have* occurred, more than once in our history, in response to moral arguments.

Viewpoint 7

"Barring notorious prisoners from the ballot box has been a staple of democracy from the Age of Pericles to the formation of the United States."

Disenfranchising Prisoners Is Just

Ben Johnson

Ben Johnson is managing editor of FrontPage Magazine, *an online publication. In the following viewpoint, he points out that Supreme Court nominee (now serving on the Court) Sonia Sotomayor wrote a minority opinion while a lower court judge in which she argued that disenfranchisement of prisoners was racially discriminatory in that the prisoners affected were disproportionately black and Hispanic. Johnson maintains that disenfranchising prisoners has a long history in the United States, is specifically permitted in the Constitution, and is not linked to racist motivations. He contends that by arguing against disenfranchisement, Sotomayor showed herself unfit to serve on the Supreme Court.*

Ben Johnson, "Sotomayor's Racialist Judicial Activism," *FrontPage Magazine*, June 26, 2009. Reproduced by permission of the author.

As you read, consider the following questions:

1. Who is Joseph "Jazz" Hayden, as described by the author?
2. What states does Johnson identify as restricting voting rights for lawbreakers in America's early history?
3. In what states today can felons vote from prison, according to the author?

Conservatives' meager attempts to navigate the difficult path opposing Sonia Sotomayor's Supreme Court nomination [by President Barack Obama in May 2009] have thus far shown their own ineptitude. Some have rightly emphasized that her statement "that a wise Latina woman with the richness of her experiences would more often than not reach a better conclusion than a white male" is reverse racism—but it hardly excites public outrage beyond the already convinced. Conservatives should recognize this and force the next stage of the public debate to revolve around a simple question: do the American people believe convicted felons in prison should have the right to vote, and that laws denying them this privilege are racist? If they disagree with both propositions, they are at odds with Sonia Sotomayor, whose positions on this and related issues demonstrate she is a judicial activist who sees the world through the lens of identity politics.

Sotomayor's position came in a terse dissent to the 2006 case *Hayden v. Pataki*. The case argued that New York's law barring convicted felons from voting until they are released from prison or complete parole is racist and thus unconstitutional. Its supporters made this argument on the grounds that "[m]ore than 80% of the New Yorkers disenfranchised . . . are Blacks or Latinos, who lose their right to vote at more than ten times the rate of other citizens." Plaintiff Joseph "Jazz" Hayden, before he began his humanitarian crusade on behalf of the disenfranchised, was convicted in 1987 of stabbing a sanitation worker to death. Most Second Circuit Court of Appeals judges disagreed with him, but Sotomayor found Hayden's objection supported by the "plain terms" of the Voting Rights Act.

Her minority opinion (no pun intended) puts into perspective precisely what a judicial activist she is and how deeply concerns of ethnicity color her view of the law.

History of Felon Disenfranchisement

Felon "disenfranchisement" is the radical idea that those imprisoned for serious infractions of the law should not be voting for those who will make it. This prudent practice has a history in the United States that predates the Constitution. Jason Schall notes in Harvard's *BlackLetter Law Journal* that the idea is as old as democracy itself, taking root in ancient Greece and continuing in Rome. The North American colonies adopted sometimes stringent regulations disqualifying antisocial voters:

> In Virginia, the franchise was denied to any "convict or person convicted in Great Britain or Ireland during the term for which he is transported." Maryland disenfranchised citizens upon their third conviction for drunkenness. . . . In Connecticut, first a majority of the town's freemen, and then the selectmen of the town, had to present a certificate as to the "honest and civil conversation" of an aspiring voter. Rhode Island required that voters be "of civil conversation [and have] acknowledged and are obedient to the civil magistrate."

Other states restricting voting rights in the nation's early history included such Jim Crow [laws that enforced racial segregation] strongholds as Ohio, Minnesota, California, and Oregon. Even [the author of *The Rich Get Richer and the Poor Get Prison* Jeffrey] Reiman concedes, "At the time of the ratification of the Fourteenth Amendment in 1868, twenty-nine states had felon disenfranchisement laws. Interestingly, in vir-

Joseph Hayden on *Hayden vs. Pataki*

The lawsuit I filed [*Hayden vs. Pataki*, in New York state,] challenges the felon disenfranchisement statutes and it challenges it in such a way that it eliminates all the discussion about debt to society and all the rest of that. We take the position that the laws are unconstitutional and that they should be swept into the dustbin of history along with the poll tax, the grandfather clause, the literacy tests, the lynch mobs, and all the rest of those obstacles to African-American empowerment in this country. And as it stands now, I filed a case—I mean a lawsuit—in the year 2000 while I was doing a term in prison and I came out and connected with the NAACP [National Association for the Advancement of Colored People] Legal Defense Fund, the Community Services Society and Center for Law and Justice. Their legal teams joined the lawsuit and we filed an amendment complaint in 2000, and it has been working its way through the district court. . . . A district judge . . . dismissed our—all our claims, you know. I mean, it was a very bad decision. And as it stands now, we're—we have decided that we're going to appeal to the Court of Appeals.

Joseph Hayden,
Democracy Now! Online, *July 9, 2004.*
www.democracynow.org.

tually all of these states, blacks had been legally denied the right to vote based on their race. Thus, the antebellum disenfranchisement statutes cannot be thought to have been racially motivated."

The second section of the 14th Amendment [which extended citizenship rights to blacks following the Civil War] specifically states voting rights should not be "in any way abridged, *except for participation in rebellion, or other crime*." In floor debates on the 14th Amendment, Representative Ephraim R. Eckley, R-OH, stated, "Under a congressional act persons convicted of a crime against the laws of the United States, the penalty for which is imprisonment in the penitentiary, are now and always have been disfranchised, and a pardon did not restore them unless the warrant of pardon so provided."

Disenfranchisement laws were later passed in a discriminatory fashion as part of Jim Crow, often openly so. However, today's voting rights milieu can hardly be called a racist dream. The vast majority of states allow felons, even violent ones like Mr. Hayden, to regain suffrage rights after completing their sentence, or finishing parole/probation. Vermont and Maine allow felons to vote from prison.

Not only has barring notorious prisoners from the ballot box been a staple of democracy from the Age of Pericles [in ancient Greece] to the formation of the United States, and not only is it specifically permitted by the U.S. Constitution, but the Supreme Court had already settled the issue. In the 1974 case *Richardson v. Ramirez*, the High Court rejected a previous challenge to such laws. William Rehnquist wrote the decision on behalf of a six-justice majority that included Warren Burger and Harry Blackmun. Will Senate Democrats grill Sotomayor over her view of *stare decisis* [the legal principle by which judges are obliged to respect earlier court decisions] as they did [chief justice] John Roberts?

Although leftists will not, Republicans should. Seeking to overturn several thousands of years of juridical precedent on the flimsiest of bases qualifies Sotomayor as a judicial activist *par excellence*, and conservatives ought not let the point go unmade because any action against this Latina will bring cries of racism. [*Editor's note: Despite the opposition, Sotomayor was confirmed and became the first Latina Supreme Court justice in August 2009.*]

> *"The fact that prisoners have a big stake in governmental choices isn't an argument in favor of disenfranchisement: it's an argument against."*

Disenfranchising Prisoners Is Unjust

Conor Clarke and Greg Yothers

Conor Clarke is an Amherst College student; Greg Yothers is an inmate at the Hampshire County Correctional Facility in Massachusetts. In the following viewpoint, the authors argue that prisoners are capable of engaging in political discussions and decisions. In addition, they maintain that since they are especially subject to government power, prisoners are especially in need of voting rights. Finally, they point out that voting helps reintegrate prisoners into citizenship. For all these reasons, the authors conclude, denying prisoners the right to vote is unjust.

As you read, consider the following questions:

1. In what year did Massachusetts disenfranchise incarcerated felons, according to the authors?

2. Why did Governor Paul Cellucci believe it was ridiculous for prisoners to organize a political action committee, in Clarke and Yothers' opinion?
3. How many prisoners do the authors say are in Massachusetts correctional facilities?

For the past 12 weeks, we have both been students in an Amherst College class on citizenship. Unlike most college courses, however, this one isn't held in a classroom. Each week, as part of the nationwide program Inside-Out, we meet for 2½ hours in the dimly lit visiting room of the Hampshire County Correctional Facility. Half the students in the class are from the college; half are inmates at the facility.

Prisoners Are Capable of Voting

It is a class on citizenship with a cruel irony: Because of a 2000 amendment to the Massachusetts constitution disenfranchising incarcerated felons, half the students in the class cannot vote. In about a week, all of the Amherst students will leave for the summer; many will volunteer for a presidential campaign. This November [2008], like most adult citizens, they will walk to a local polling station or cast absentee ballots from the comfort of a college dorm. The students inside the facility can't.

American incarceration has received a lot of attention recently. [In February 2008], *The New York Times* reported that one in every 100 American adults is in prison, the highest rate in the world by a wide margin, and about six times higher than the world median. This drive to incarcerate has been rightly and roundly criticized as too expensive (it costs more per capita to imprison than educate) and too harsh, since the vast majority of inmates are serving time for nonviolent crimes. But amid the controversy over price and punishment, it tends to be forgotten that incarceration imposes a cost on American democracy: The more we imprison, the less we vote.

Enfranchising Felons in Florida

By 2007, Florida had disenfranchised 950,000 citizens who had felony convictions—the vast majority of whom were Black, Latino, and low-income people. In an unexpected move, Florida Republican Governor Charlie Crist changed his anti-felon position, to declare that the time had come . . . to leave the "offensive minority" of states that uniformly denied ex-prisoners voting rights. [In] April 2007, Governor Crist persuaded Florida's clemency board to restore voting rights to about 800,000 former prisoners.

Manning Marable,
Black Star News, *April 9, 2007.*
www.blackstarnews.com.

Why should that be the case? In early 2000, before the amendment passed, [Massachusetts] Governor Paul Cellucci told Bryant Gumbel of CBS News that disenfranchisement was necessary to ensure that felons did not damage the political process. Cellucci said, after a group of Massachusetts prisoners tried to organize a political action committee in 1997, he "thought that this was a little bit ridiculous, that prisoners would actually politically organize and try to lobby against the very laws that put them in prison to protect the people of this state." The clear implication was that, once you've broken the social contract, you've proved yourself unfit for any social contact, including the right to vote.

But our experience in class suggests that the opposite is true. We all write the same papers, read the same material by John Locke and Alexis de Tocqueville [political philosophers known for their roles in formulating democratic political theory], and are all equally engaged in debating and discussing everything from the role of the good citizen to America's role in the world. There is no reason to think inmates are uniquely unqualified to wield a vote, and no reason to think they can't.

Prisoners Need to Vote

Yes, going to prison necessarily entails the loss of liberty. But the right to vote is in many ways more important than the right to walk freely down the street: Voting is the most basic check against the coercive power of the state. The places where that coercive power is most starkly exercised, such as prisons, are also the places where that most basic of checks becomes more important. The fact that prisoners have a big stake in governmental choices isn't an argument in favor of disenfranchisement; it's an argument against.

And because the vote is so essential to democratic citizenship, it is also an important part of reintegrating inmates with society. Prisons separate and divide, but at their best they also prepare inmates for life after imprisonment. Rebuilding civic engagement is perhaps the most important part of that process.

There are more than 25,000 inmates in Massachusetts correctional facilities, and more than half are racial minorities. Almost all of them will, at some point in the future, exit their cells and return to their homes and families. It would be better if they returned as voting citizens.

Periodical Bibliography

The following articles have been selected to supplement the diverse views presented in this chapter.

Lee P. Brown	"Two Takes: Drugs Are a Major Social Problem, We Cannot Legalize Them," *U.S. News & World Report*, July 25, 2008.
Jason DeParle	"The American Prison Nightmare," *New York Review of Books*, April 12, 2007.
Glenn Greenwald	"Jim Webb's Courage v. the 'Pragmatism' Excuse for Politicians," *Salon*, March 28, 2009. www.salon.com.
John R. Lott Jr.	"Reforms That Ignore the Black Victims of Crime," *Cato Unbound*, March 13, 2009. www.cato-unbound.org.
Jonathan Meador	"From Prison to the Voting Booth," *LEO Weekly*, September 30, 2009.
Amanda Paulson	"Poll: 60 Percent of Americans Oppose Mandatory Minimum Sentences," *Christian Science Monitor*, September 25, 2008.
Bradford Polumer	"The Prison Dilemma," *New Republic*, October 1, 2007.
John H. Richardson	"A Radical Solution to End the Drug War: Legalize *Everything*," *Esquire*, September 1, 2009.
U.S. Courts	"Inflexible Mandatory Minimum Statutes Often Create Unjust Results," July 14, 2009. www.uscourts.gov.
Bruce Western	"Race, Crime, and Punishment," *Cato Unbound*, March 18, 2009. www.cato-unbound.org.
James Q. Wilson	"Addressing the Problems That Lead to Prison," *Cato Unbound*, March 16, 2009. www.cato-unbound.org.

CHAPTER 3

Are American Prisons Humane?

Chapter Preface

America is one of the few Western democracies that has a death penalty. Those who are awaiting capital punishment are generally placed in a special section of the prison called death row. As of January 1, 2009, there were 3,297 prisoners awaiting execution in the United States, according to the Death Penalty Information Center.

Many activists have maintained that conditions for death row inmates are often inhumane. The Death Penalty Information Center (DPIC) argues this case on a Web page titled "Time on Death Row." According to the organization, most death row inmates spend more than ten years waiting to be executed, and some wait for more than twenty years. While they are being held, DPIC says, "they are generally isolated from other prisoners, excluded from prison education programs, and sharply restricted in terms of visitation and exercise, spending as much as twenty-three hours a day alone in their cells." DPIC then notes that "this raises the question of whether death row prisoners are receiving two distinct punishments: the death sentence itself, and the years of living in conditions tantamount to solitary confinement—a severe form of punishment that may be used only for very limited periods for general-population prisoners."

Conditions on death row can be harsh even beyond the isolation. In a report from the Reuters news service on January 7, 2002, Alan Elsner reported that on death row in Texas, men were "held in solitary confinement, given rotten food to eat, deprived of sleep and often subjected to salvos of pepper spray by guards." The Texas Coalition to Abolish the Death Penalty alleged that one prisoner died of a heart attack after guards denied him medical help for two days. Similarly, a Florida death row prisoner named Mike Lambrix stated in a blog post on November 10, 2008, that "I have been on Florida's death row now for about 25 years. . . . In my personal experience I can tell you that the conditions we must 'live' under far exceed any objective definition of 'cruel and unusual' punishment." Lambrix claimed that death row prisoners were kept in solitary confinement and that the food they were provided was inedible.

Others have argued that death row inmates may exaggerate the harshness of the conditions they live under. For example, a Texas Department of Corrections spokesman named Larry Fitzgerald told Alan Elsner that the meals served to the death row inmates were the same as those served to officers, and noted "I eat them myself." In addition, some believe that prisoners on death row can occasionally be treated too well. Bryan Robinson, writing for ABC News online on May 28, 2004, reported that Oregon convicted murderer and death row prisoner Horacio Alberto Reyes-Camarena was to be placed on a list to receive a kidney transplant. If Reyes-Camarena received a kidney, it would necessarily deprive another citizen of that organ. Joshua Marqui, Oregon district attorney, noted that the state was legally bound to provide health care for its prisoners, but added, "'Personally, I find it abhorrent that someone like Mr. Reyes-Camarena could receive a transplant before anybody who is more deserving.'"

As these arguments demonstrate, the state is often reluctant to spend taxpayer money in order to provide services for those who have committed crimes when those same dollars could be spent on services for the law-abiding. At the same time, the state is responsible for the well-being of those in its care, and there is a constitutional duty not to impose cruel punishment. These factors affect not just death row inmates, but all prisoners. The authors of the viewpoints in the following chapter debate the humaneness of America's prisons.

VIEWPOINT 1

> *"We expect our correctional staff to treat inmates fairly and with respect."*

American Prisons Are Humane

Harley G. Lappin

Harley G. Lappin is director of the Federal Bureau of Prisons. In the following viewpoint, he contends that the Federal Bureau of Prisons is dedicated to the humane and fair treatment of prisoners. He asserts that the bureau exceeds the standards put forward in the U.S. Constitution and that it welcomes and learns from regulatory oversight. Lappin also maintains that there are procedures in place to ensure that prisoners with complaints or who feel that their safety is threatened can report problems and have their concerns addressed.

As you read, consider the following questions:

1. According to Lappin, how does the bureau ensure direct and effective communication with inmates?
2. What external audit authorities have ongoing interest in bureau operations, according to the author?

Harley G. Lappin, "Statement of Harley G. Lappin, Director, Federal Bureau of Prisons, Before the Commission on Safety and Abuse in America's Prisons," Commission on Safety and Abuse in America's Prisons Web Site, February 9, 2006.

3. To what agency are allegations of staff misconduct referred, according to Lappin?

I would like to provide a brief overview of the Federal Bureau of Prisons' internal, self-imposed oversight and accountability procedures designed to help us optimally accomplish our mission's two objectives: the safe, secure, and humane confinement of those entrusted to our care, and facilitating successful, crime-free re-entry for those released back to the community.

Fair Treatment

First, let me set the stage by discussing pertinent Bureau philosophy. The Bureau has been well-served by our core values which include "recognizing the inherent dignity of all human beings and their potential for positive change." We expect our correctional staff to treat inmates fairly and with respect. The Bureau further recognizes that offenders are incarcerated *as* punishment, not *for* punishment. All Bureau of Prisons staff share a common role as correctional worker, which requires taking responsibility for maintaining safe and secure institutions and for modeling society's mainstream values and norms. Bureau staff are expected to serve as a positive example for inmates to emulate in preparing for a crime-free return to the community after release. These core values are deeply ingrained in the Bureau culture and repeated to staff often beginning with the staff training provided to new hires and reinforced annually through refresher training.

Another key factor that contributes to safe and secure inmate management is direct and effective communication with inmates. Staff are highly visible throughout the institution and readily available to address inmate concerns or questions at the lowest level, thus proactively preventing potential problems from escalating. Unit team staff members, who work most closely with inmates assigned to them, have offices in the inmate housing units to provide ready access, as well as inmate supervision; institution executive staff, including the Warden and Associate Wardens, department heads, and unit team members are highly visible and provide coverage of the dining room during meal times; and key personnel make regular visits to the Special Housing Unit to provide inmates in disciplinary segregation with access to avenues for problem identification and resolution. These are just some examples of processes in place for inmate protection.

Exceeding Standards

While the U.S. Constitution, along with Federal and state laws, establishes minimum standards of care to which all inmates are entitled, the Bureau has always worked, over its more than 75-year history, to achieve the highest of standards with respect to inmate management. Bureau staff work diligently every day to meet clearly-defined performance expectations; and that collective effort has earned the agency a leadership role in the field of corrections. However, we fully recognize that the Bureau's reputation can only be maintained through the continued dedication to public service, professionalism, and exceptional performance of its staff.

Certainly many external audit authorities have ongoing interest in Bureau operations and programs for regulatory oversight, including Congress, the Government Accounting Office, and the Department of Justice's Office of Inspector General. We take our role as stewards of the public's trust very seriously and welcome the scrutiny. The Bureau uses the results from these external audits to improve operations.

Beyond externally-mandated oversight, the Bureau is a policy driven agency with numerous built-in mechanisms of critical self-review and management control. The provisions outlined in policy regarding internal systems of control apply to all Bureau organizational components and sites, including Central Office divisions, regional offices, institutions, and

The Annual Suicide Rate in the Bureau of Prisons, 1990–2004

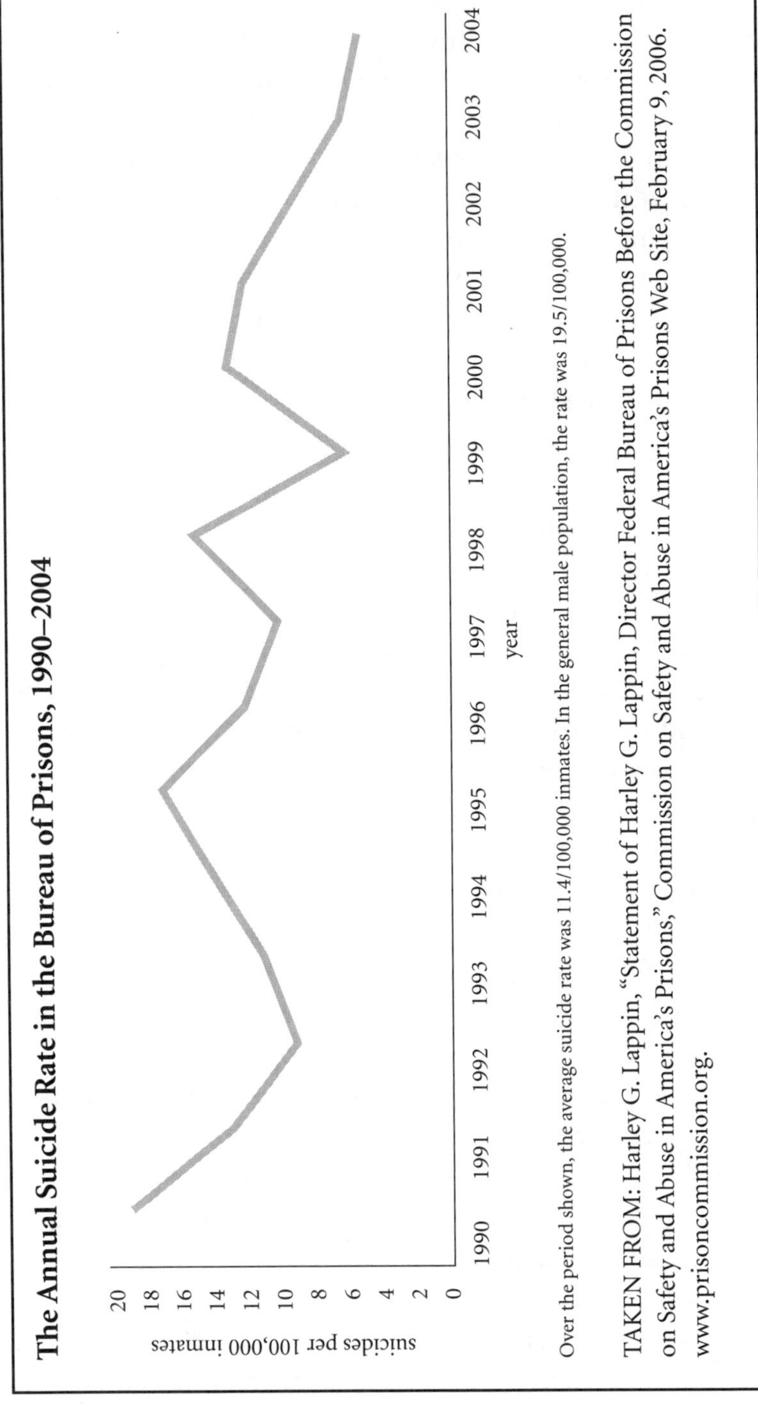

Over the period shown, the average suicide rate was 11.4/100,000 inmates. In the general male population, the rate was 19.5/100,000.

TAKEN FROM: Harley G. Lappin, "Statement of Harley G. Lappin, Director Federal Bureau of Prisons Before the Commission on Safety and Abuse in America's Prisons," Commission on Safety and Abuse in America's Prisons Web Site, February 9, 2006. www.prisoncommission.org.

community corrections offices, and also extend to the Bureau's oversight of private contract facilities. Contractors dealing with inmates (such as halfway house providers or privately-managed secure facilities housing Bureau inmates) and their operations are closely monitored by Bureau staff to ensure compliance with all applicable standards.

The Bureau's internal systems of checks and balances are designed to achieve various objectives, including but not restricted to the following: ensuring compliance with applicable regulations, laws, policies, and procedures; monitoring vital functions and operations; identifying weaknesses and enhancements needed; promoting efficient management practices; determining whether programs are achieving desired results; and enhancing program quality. Incorporating information from various sources results in a Bureau management approach that is holistic and comprehensive in nature. . . .

Inmates Have Remedies

The Administrative Remedy Program is an internal grievance process through which an inmate may request consideration or review of any issue related to their conditions of confinement. The inmate must first present an issue of concern informally to staff, and staff must attempt to informally resolve the issue before an inmate submits a formal request for Administrative Remedy. By policy, each institution has established procedures for informally resolving inmate complaints.

If the inmate views the issue as sensitive and is concerned that his/her safety or well-being would be compromised if the request became known at the institution, the inmate may submit the request directly to the Regional Director. If the request is determined to be of an emergency nature which threatens the inmate's immediate health or welfare, the Warden (or Regional Director) must respond promptly. The program requires timely investigation and response, including redress as appropriate. Procedures are in place for inmates and members of the public to request access to Administrative Remedy indexes (or entry/status logs) and responses, from which inmate names and register numbers have been removed.

All allegations of staff misconduct, including allegations that a staff member has abused an inmate, are referred to the OIG [Office of the Inspector General] which then refers back to the Bureau's organizationally independent Office of Internal Affairs (OIA) those they want the Bureau to investigate. The OIG also has a hotline available to the public for reporting any Department of Justice employee they believe has violated their civil rights or civil liberties. The Bureau takes all allegations of staff misconduct and mistreatment very seriously and investigates every allegation thoroughly. We do not tolerate any type of abuse of inmates. When allegations of serious abuse are accompanied by credible evidence, the staff member is removed from contact with inmates or placed on administrative leave. We refer serious cases of staff misconduct for criminal prosecution when warranted.

The Bureau of Prisons is fortunate to have relatively few major incidents at our facilities—homicides, escapes, suicides, use of lethal force. Serious assaults or incidents that have criminal implications are referred to the Federal Bureau of Investigation for prosecution. Additionally, follow-ups of each such incident with "After-action reviews" are conducted by senior level staff from other Bureau sites to examine what occurred leading up to the event(s) and offer recommendations based on the findings to ensure any possible breakdowns or lapses are not repeated. Findings are shared with the appropriate senior level managers so that lessons learned can benefit the agency as a whole.

Viewpoint 2

"Overcrowding—having more prisoners than a facility can accommodate in a psychologically healthy and humane way—is directly connected to many of the problems that currently confront American corrections."

Overcrowding in American Prisons Is Inhumane

Craig Haney

Craig Haney is a professor of psychology at the University of California, Santa Cruz, and author of Reforming Punishment: Psychological Limits to the Pains of Imprisonment. *In the following viewpoint, he argues that overcrowding in prisons puts inmates under painful stress and reduces the services available to them. He also maintains that the overcrowding encourages the prison administration to focus on harsh and inhumane means of discipline in order to maintain control over the large number of inmates.*

As you read, consider the following questions:

1. What are the two largest state prison systems in the nation, according to the author?

Craig Haney, "Prison Overcrowding: Harmful Consequences and Dysfunctional Reactions," Commission on Safety and Abuse in America's Prisons Web Site. Reproduced by permission of the author.

2. According to Haney, what factors contribute to an increase in prison rape?
3. What does the author say is perhaps the most punitive correctional trend?

The massive influx of prisoners that began in the late 1970s and early 1980s in the United States produced a rate of growth in the nation's prison population that scholars and legal commentators have repeatedly characterized as "unprecedented." Among other things, this unprecedented prison growth meant that systems everywhere were dangerously overcrowded—and many still are. In fact, some prison systems grew so large, so quickly, that it became difficult for prison officials to keep track of the names and locations of all of the facilities in their system, let alone to meaningfully supervise and oversee them.

The two largest prison systems in the nation—California and Texas—experienced comparable, remarkable rates of rapid growth. Over the last 30 years, California's prisoner population expanded eightfold (from roughly 20,000 in the early 1970s to its current [2006] population of approximately 160,000 prisoners). Funding for prisoner services and programming did not remotely keep pace, which meant that many more prisoners had to make do on much less. In Texas, over just the brief five-year period between 1992 and 1997, the prisoner population more than doubled as nearly 70,000 additional prisoners were added to the prison rolls. Indeed, during the mid-1990s Texas achieved one of the highest incarceration rates in the nation, and the state now operates more than 80 prisons in order to accommodate the expansion in its already sizable prisoner population.

Risking Organizational Stability

Of course, systems that grow at such a pace are at risk of losing their organizational stability. Despite the rate at which correctional capacity has been increased, many prison systems remain significantly overcrowded. Overcrowding, in turn, exacerbates the chronic pains of imprisonment. Not surprisingly, a large literature on overcrowding has documented a range of adverse effects that occur when prisons have been filled to capacity and beyond. As a group of prison researchers summarized in the 1980s, as the problem was just beginning to take shape, "crowding in prisons is a major source of administrative problems and adversely affects inmate health, behavior, and morale." . . .

Although other variables may mediate or reduce the negative effects of crowding, the psychological toll can be substantial. Thus, despite an occasional study that yields an inconclusive finding, there is little reason to doubt the empirical consensus that crowding significantly worsens the quality of institutional life and increases the destructive potential of imprisonment. Among other things, we know that prison overcrowding increases negative affect among prisoners, elevates their blood pressure, and leads to greater numbers of prisoner illness complaints. Not surprisingly, exposure to "long-term, intense, inescapable crowding" of the sort that now characterizes many prison environments results in high levels of stress that "can lead to physical and psychological impairment." In addition, overcrowding has been associated with higher rates of disciplinary infractions. For example, one study concluded that in prisons "where crowded conditions are chronic rather than temporary . . . there is a clear association between restrictions on personal space and the occurrence of disciplinary violations."

Overcrowding directly affects prisoners' mental and physical health by increasing the level of uncertainty with which they regularly must cope. One useful psychological model of the negative effects of overcrowding emphasizes the way in which being confined in a space that is occupied by too many people increases the sheer number of social interactions per-

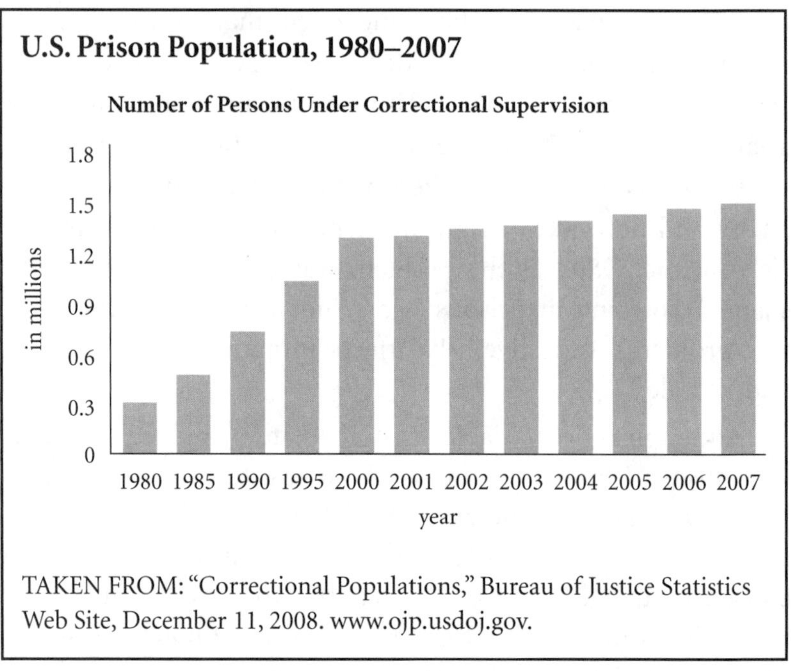

TAKEN FROM: "Correctional Populations," Bureau of Justice Statistics Web Site, December 11, 2008. www.ojp.usdoj.gov.

sons have that involve "high levels of uncertainty, goal interference, and cognitive load . . ." Thus, crowded conditions heighten the level of cognitive strain that persons experience by introducing social complexity, turnover, and interpersonal instability into an already dangerous prison world in which interpersonal mistakes or errors in social judgments can be fatal. Of course, overcrowding also raises collective frustration levels inside prisons by generally decreasing the resources available to the prisoners confined in them. The sheer number of things prisoners do or accomplish on a day-to-day basis is compromised by the amount of people in between them and their goals and destinations.

Overcrowding Is Dangerous

Prisoners in overcrowded correctional settings interact with more unfamiliar people, under extremely close quarters that afford little or no privacy or respite, where their basic needs are less likely to be addressed or met. Indeed, overcrowding operates at an individual level to worsen the experience of imprisonment by literally changing the social context or situation to which prisoners must adapt on a day-to-day basis. In addition to these direct, individual level effects, however, overcrowding changes the way the prison itself functions.

For one, prison systems responding to the press of numbers often forego the careful screening, monitoring, and managing of vulnerable or problematic prisoners—in part because there are too many of them to assess in a conscientious way and in part because the system lacks the capacity to address their special needs anyway. As one group of clinicians conceded, "Unfortunately, the prospect of screening inmates for mental disorder and treating those in need of mental health services has become a daunting and nearly impossible task in the present explosion of prison growth." Unidentified and untreated mentally ill prisoners in mainline prison populations not only are more likely to deteriorate themselves, but also to have a significant adverse effect on the prisoners with whom they must live and interact.

Over the last several decades, prison administrators reacted to unprecedented levels of overcrowding in a variety of ways that—no doubt quite unintentionally—altered the nature of the prison settings—indeed, often made prison a more painful, harmful, and even more dangerous place. For example, resources for already limited programming and other activities were reallocated to create bedspace and maintain basic security. As the Commission [on Safety and Abuse in America's Prisons] no doubt knows, the prison overcrowding crisis in the United States coincided with the advent of a correctional philosophy that saw deprivation as a goal rather than a problem. Unprecedented amounts of unproductive inactivity and idleness resulted. . . .

There is widespread agreement among correctional experts that chronic idleness produces negative psychological and behavioral effects in prison. As far back as the 1980s, when trends toward overcrowding and the lack of prison programming had just begun, the U.S. Government Accounting Office noted, "Corrections officials believe that extensive inmate idleness can lead to destructive behavior and increase violence within institutions. Moreover, idleness does little to prepare inmates for re-entry into society." But this warning was largely ignored as the trends toward higher rates of incarceration intensified over the next several decades.

Idleness-related frustration increases the probability of interpersonal conflict and assaults in prison. Overcrowding simultaneously reduces the opportunities for staff to effectively monitor prisoner behavior and drastically limits the options to reduce animosities between prisoners by separating them or sending them to different facilities. Thus, there is less for prisoners to do, fewer outlets to release the resulting tension, a decreased staff capacity to identify prisoner problems, and fewer options to solve them if and when they do. Among the negative behavioral effects that are likely to occur is an increased risk of victimization. For example, one prison researcher has noted that "[i]n less well-regulated institutions in which prisoners have little recourse to protection or in which there may be collusion between dominant prisoners and staff to maintain the peace, sexual violence tends to be greater." Others agreed that overcrowded conditions in which prisoners have much idle time can contribute to a higher level of prison rapes. . . .

Force and Intimidation

Overcrowding, widespread idleness, and the failure of many prison systems to address the basic needs of prisoners have changed the context of imprisonment. Prison administrators have been forced to anticipate and react to many volatile and potentially explosive situations. In many instances, their reactions have been predictable but problematic, serving to increase the amount of prison pain dispensed and making already dangerous situations, in the long run, more so.

Indeed, in the face of extraordinary increases in the sheer numbers of prisoners, many prison administrators pressed for new tools with which to control and contain them. In most jurisdictions, any pretense of carefully managing the prison "careers" of inmates or effectively monitoring the quality of the conditions under which they were kept was sacrificed during the rapid expansion of the prisoner population. Criminologists Malcolm Feeley and Jonathan Simon identified an emerging penological management style in which correctional decision makers now think about prisoners only in the "aggregate," as dangerous "populations" that need to be "herded," rather than as individuals in need of personal attention. Indeed, in terms that captured both the dehumanized consciousness of the decision makers, and the devalued status of the prisoners under their control, Feeley and Simon analogized the overcrowding-driven new penology as akin to a "waste management" function.

Thus, rather than improving living conditions and investing in prison programs and meaningful activities in which prisoners could participate, many prison systems have committed to harsh policies and procedures designed primarily to maintain order and control and little else. They also now rely increasingly on sophisticated and expensive security hardware and surveillance technology. Metal detectors, x-ray machines, leg irons, waist chains, handcuffs, "black boxes" [designed to immobilize the hands and prevent the inmate from picking the handcuff lock], holding cages, "violent prisoner restraint chairs," psychiatric screens, chain-link fences, concertina wire, tasers, stun guns, pepper spray, tear gas canisters, gas grenades, and, in some jurisdictions, mini-14 and 9 millimeter rifles, 12 gauge shotguns, and the like now are employed inside the cellblocks of a number of maximum security prisons.

For example, in maximum security prisons in California, guards armed with rifles are strategically positioned inside mainline housing units and authorized to respond to inmate disturbances with lethal force. Even when they are asleep, prisoners are under what is euphemistically called "gun cover." In New York City, the city's large jail on Rikers Island has resorted to what has been characterized [by Feeley and Simon] as an "iron hand" approach to regain and maintain order by "[u]sing an array of tools and tactics—from a huge S.W.A.T. [special weapons and tactics] team to electric stun shields to a program that aggressively prosecutes inmates for crimes committed inside the jail." . . .

In perhaps the most punitive correctional trend, many prison systems are making more extensive use of a new form of disciplinary segregation or "lockup." The use of long-term solitary confinement that was tried and then abandoned in the 19th century—when its psychological effects were recognized as harmful and inhumane—has returned in the last several decades of the 20th century, in the form of the modern "supermax" prison. Presumably designed to limit and control violence by keeping prisoners isolated from one another, the practice confines them under especially harsh and deprived conditions for very long periods of time, with potentially disastrous psychological consequences. Despite judicial rulings that have severely criticized these practices, courts have permitted prison systems to continue to employ them.

As I have tried to show, overcrowding—having more prisoners than a facility can accommodate in a psychologically healthy and humane way—is directly connected to many of the problems that currently confront American corrections. Although it is by no means the only cause of the sometimes dangerous conditions and potential for abuse that exists in many of our nation's prisons, it is a central and critical issue that must be effectively addressed if these other problems are to be solved.

Viewpoint 3

> *"Since Tasers were introduced to the jail . . . jail officials say there have been far fewer disturbances between inmates and officers."*

Stun Technology Makes Prisons Safer

Jeff Wiehe

Jeff Wiehe is a reporter for the Journal Gazette *newspaper of Fort Wayne, Indiana. In the following viewpoint, he reports on the use of Tasers, or stun guns, at the Allen County Jail in Indiana. According to Wiehe, the use of Tasers has reduced violent incidents at the jail and made prisoners more cooperative. Wiehe also reports that Taser use is closely monitored and regulated, and that in most cases simply the threat of Taser use can defuse a potentially violent situation.*

As you read, consider the following questions:

1. According to the author, do officials at Allen County Jail have records to support their claim that Tasers have reduced violent incidents with inmates?
2. According to Wiehe, what is a dry stun?

Jeff Wiehe, "Tasers Touted As Effective Tool," *Journal Gazette*, October 26, 2008. Reproduced by permission.

3. Why are handguns not allowed in Allen County Jail, in the author's view?

Andrew Keller took the bright yellow X-26 model Taser from his belt, pointed it to the ground one afternoon this month and made it cackle like a rattlesnake, testing to make sure it worked properly.

"If you've ever been tased, that sound will make the hair on the back of your neck stand straight up," said Keller, a confinement officer at the Allen County Jail.

He should know. To complete his training and become authorized to use the weapon, Keller had to be shot with the Taser. He's now one of several confinement officers who can choose to carry any of the six Tasers the jail has available during a given shift.

Tasers Encourage Cooperation

Inmates also know about the weapons.

Since Tasers were introduced to the jail nearly a year ago, jail officials say there have been far fewer disturbances between inmates and officers, far fewer situations where officers had to get physical with inmates, and far fewer uncooperative inmates—an attitude adjustment they attribute to having the non-lethal weapon at their disposal.

Jail officials could provide only anecdotal evidence because they don't have records readily available to tell whether incidents at the jail are down. Not every situation at the jail requires a report or is documented, such as minor incidents where an officer might have to put his hands on an inmate to move him or her into a cell.

Jail Commander Charles Hart said there's a sense of less violence in the jail, and he claims fewer people report incidents to him, though he can't give exact numbers.

"There's no real way we can gauge it," Hart said.

Infrequently Used

The devices used at the jail—built by Taser International—have two prongs that can be shot into a person from 15 feet away to deliver a charge of electricity that incapacitates an inmate. Though warning posters for inmates at the jail indicate the gun carries a charge of 50,000 volts, Taser International claims the actual voltage goes down to 1,200 volts as the charge hits the body, then lowers more as it enters the body.

A "dry stun" from the Tasers can also be administered for "pain compliance," according to the sheriff's department. A dry stun is delivered by putting the end of the weapon against the person's body, which gives a shock drastically weaker than the prongs.

So far, Tasers have been shot at inmates nine times in the jail and used in dry stuns 11 times.

The first dry stun came the day Tasers were brought into the jail—Nov. 22, 2007. A woman housed in a cell reserved for suicidal inmates kept putting wet toilet paper over the camera so officers couldn't see her. When officers tried to remove her from the cell, she hid under her bunk and resisted their attempts to carry her out, according to a police report.

After giving her several warnings, one of the officers used a Taser to give the woman a quick shock, and she then complied with their commands.

"If you have to put your hands on an inmate to force them to do something, to physically control them, you can tase them," sheriff's department spokesman Sergeant Steve Stone said in explaining the department's Taser policy.

For example, on March 5, an inmate causing a disturbance refused to come out of his cell when ordered and challenged an officer to a fight.

"Come on then and get (expletive) up," the inmate apparently told the officer while he clenched his fists, according to a police report. The officer warned the inmate he had a Taser, but the inmate still refused to come out and kept himself in a "combative stance."

After several more warnings, the officer shot the Taser's prongs into the inmate's chest.

Every time an officer uses the weapon, he or she must file a report. Those reports and incidents are reviewed at least quarterly—sooner if they begin to pile up—to make sure the weapons were used correctly in every instance, according to Captain Ron Rayl of the sheriff's Internal Affairs Division.

Most of the incidents involving Tasers have been justified, according to the department. One officer in February, however, was disciplined for improper use of a Taser when he shocked a female inmate twice, the second time unnecessarily, according to Rayl. That officer was suspended without pay for two days, could not use a Taser for a period of time, and was given remedial training on how to use the weapon.

There is also a civil tort claim, suggesting a lawsuit is in the works, for a separate incident involving a Taser in the jail, according to Rayl. No officers were punished in that case.

"I'd like it to be zero, of course, for us to have none," Sheriff Ken Fries said about the incident that required punishment to an officer. "But I think this should bode well for us in that we noticed it and took care of it. We don't expect it to happen again."

The Tasers at the jail have a video camera attached that automatically turns on when used. But the department also wanted to track how effective the threat of Tasers are in getting inmates to cooperate.

Even Threats of Tasing Reported

Every time an officer uses one to threaten an inmate—either by reaching for it or taking it out and aiming it—he or she is required to fill out a memo for the sheriff's department's Special Operations and Training staff.

Stun Gun Technology

In recent years, electro-muscular-disruption technology—also known as conducted-energy devices (CEDs) or stun guns or by the trade name Taser—has become the less-lethal device of choice for a growing number of law enforcement agencies. CEDs use a high-voltage, low-power charge of electricity to induce involuntary muscle contractions that cause temporary incapacitation. . . .

Researchers at the University of Wisconsin found that CEDs can directly "electrocute" the heart rhythm, although the chance of this happening is quite small. . . . Research published in 2007 shows that CEDs can cause heart fibrillation (a dangerously disturbed heart rhythm) in people with pacemakers. . . .

One concern with CEDs has been that they cause involuntary muscle contractions and thus might cause muscle breakdown, changes in blood chemistry, and perhaps resulting heart failure. Physiological testing has not shown significant signs that these problems actually occur.

John Morgan,
Office of Justice Programs Web site,
October 27, 2008. www.ojp.usdoj.gov.

That's happened 26 times at the jail, and each time, inmates obeyed officers, according to the sheriff's department.

Anthony A. Parish, a 19-year-old suspected "D-Boys" gang member facing an attempted murder charge, was refusing officers' orders to dress in a special uniform showing he's being kept in protective custody on October 16, according to one of the memos.

"(Officer) advised Parish that he needed to get dressed and that if he refused to get dressed, all officers present would have to assist him," the memo said.

When Parish refused again, one of the officers took out his Taser, aimed it at Parish and trained a red laser light from the weapon on his chest. "Inmate Parish then stated that he would get dressed," the memo said.

"When you draw it, it's an instant attitude change," said Keller, who has been a confinement officer for eight years. "There's been a noticeable difference. It's a huge deterrent. Just by reaching for it, that's usually all it takes."

And that's what officials were hoping would happen with the Tasers—fewer altercations, less physical interaction between inmates and officers.

"The entire reason to get Tasers was to save injuries to both suspects and officers," Fries said. "As police, we're always seeking voluntary compliance, and hopefully just the threat of a Taser would lead to voluntary compliance."

Handguns are not allowed in the jail for safety reasons, and Fries had a concern about Tasers, fearing that an inmate might try to take one away from an officer. That hasn't happened so far, he said.

There have been reports across the country of deaths after Tasers were fired, with many questioning the devices' safety, but no deaths have occurred from their use at the Allen County Jail.

"If I didn't think they were safe, they wouldn't be there," Fries said. "I think the officers are more secure, the inmates are safer."

VIEWPOINT 4

> *"Electronic [shocking] devices . . . may cause heart attack, ventricular fibrillation, or arrhythmia."*

Stun Technology Is Inhumane and Dangerous

Anne-Marie Cusac

Anne-Marie Cusac is an award-winning investigative journalist and an assistant professor in the Department of Communication at Roosevelt University in Chicago. In the following viewpoint, she argues that stun technology in general, and stun belts developed by a company called Stun Tech in particular, are dangerous and potentially deadly. Cusac notes that there is evidence that the belts can cause heart failure and death. She argues that claims that the technology is medically safe are untested and unwarranted.

As you read, consider the following questions:

1. As the author reports, what did Stun Tech change its name to?
2. Who was Harry Landis, and why is his story useful to Cusac's viewpoint?

Anne-Marie Cusac, *Cruel and Unusual: Punishment in America*, New Haven, CT: Yale University Press, 2009.

3. According to the author, what international committee has asked the United States to ban use of the stun belt?

In the 1990s a company called Stun Tech invented the REACT (Remote Electronically Activated Control Technology) belt. An electronic shocking device secured to a person's waist, the belt was the hot new item in corrections gear. The device appealed to guards because they could apply punishment without having to go near the prisoner wearing the belt. They could set off the eight-second, 50,000-volt stun from as far away as three hundred feet.

Stun Tech claimed the device was "100 percent non-lethal." Sales boomed in 1994 when the federal Bureau of Prisons decided to use the belt in medium- and high-security lockups. By 1996, the U.S. Marshals Service, more than one hundred county agencies, and sixteen state correctional agencies employed the belt for prisoner transport, courtroom appearances, and medical appointments. By 2002, the manufacturer, now known as Electronic Defense Technology (EDT), claimed it had sold 1,900 belts, which had been worn more than 65,000 times by prisoners across the country. . . .

Heart Trouble

According to two physicians and a 1990 study by the British Forensic Science Service, electronic devices similar to the belt may cause heart attack, ventricular fibrillation, or arrhythmia, and may set off an adverse reaction in people with epilepsy or on psychotropic medications. Stun Tech denied that its belt could cause fatalities. . . .

In 1995, a Texas corrections officer suffered a heart attack shortly after receiving a shock from an electric shield similar in design to the stun belt. Like many other Texas corrections workers, Harry Landis was in training to use the electric riot shield. Like the stun belt, the taser, and the stun gun, the shield is an electronic shocking device. Guards frequently use the shield when removing prisoners from their cells. But on December 1, 1995, something went terribly wrong. As part of the training, Landis was required to endure two 45,000-volt shocks. Shortly after the second shock, Landis collapsed and died.

The Texas Department of Criminal Justice, which had used the shields to subdue prisoners since September 1995, immediately suspended their use. The maker of the shield denied that it had killed Landis: "We're very sorry this happened," said John McDermit, president of Nova Products, Inc., "but there certainly was no connection between his training and his death."

Jimmy Wood, the Coryell County justice of the peace who conducted an inquiry into Landis's death, tells a different story. "Landis was in fairly decent shape as far as physical appearance is concerned," he says. "He did have a history of heart problems. But was he going to die this day if he didn't experience an electric shock? No, he wasn't." According to Jimmy Wood, Landis's autopsy showed that he died as a result of cardiac dirhythmia due to coronary blockage following electric shock by an electronic stun shield. "The electric shock threw his heart into a different rhythmic beat, causing him to pass away."

"The shield worked as it was intended to," says Mark Goodson, an engineer who conducted tests on the shield following Landis's death. "Now comes the problem. The manufacturer puts in its literature that the shield will not hurt anyone, including people with a heart condition. But they have not done studies on people with heart conditions. They haven't done studies on people at all. They conducted their tests on animals—anesthetized animals. Do you see the danger here? In one word: adrenaline." Goodson explains that this is a problem with all pulsed electrical stun technology. "No one can even define a safe voltage. . . . We don't even have an idea if it is safe or not for the general population." . . .

Odds of Dying by Stun Gun

The chance of dying after being shot by a taser or stun gun is about one in 870. Dr. William P. Bozeman . . . estimates this in the September 2005 issue of the *Annals of Emergency Medicine.*

But Dr. Bozeman acknowledges that any such estimate is based on very little data. Tasers and stun guns have been in use for only a short period of time and there are still few studies assessing their various effects.

Stephen Juan,
Register *(UK), October 13, 2006.*
www.theregister.co.uk.

Dangerous Shocks

A 1990 study by the British Forensic Science Service, a British government agency . . . found that high-voltage, high-peak, short-duration pulses, such as those the stun belt inflicts, are dangerous. The study describes stun devices as "capable of causing temporary incapacitation of the whole body: a body-widespread immobilizing effect." A one-to-two-second shock, noted the scientists, would probably cause the victim to collapse. A three-to-four-second shock would have an incapacitating effect on the entire body for up to fifteen minutes. Since the shock is distributed via electric currents throughout the entire body, including the brain, the chest region and the central nervous system, the researchers concluded that "anyone in contact with the victim's body at the time of shocking was also likely to receive a shock," and that they "could not discount the possibility of ventricular fibrillation." This is to say that a stun device could kill someone.

Although Stun Tech advised guards not to use the belt on inmates with a known heart condition, this precaution hardly eliminates all potential dangers. For one thing, some at-risk hearts appear healthy. "You shock someone with 50,000 volts of electricity and that person has some unrecognized congenital problem or conduction mechanism in their heart, and you put them at great risk for arrhythmia," said Armond Start, a medical doctor and former head of the National Center for Correctional Healthcare Studies. "You can't predict this. You can't determine the conduction mechanism in a heart. Arrhythmia mostly happens in healthy hearts."

Starl questioned Electronic Defense Technology's claims that the belt is medically safe. When he served as medical director of the Texas state prison system, stun guns, closely related to the belts, were being employed. The state eventually stopped using them. "Having dealt with the stun gun, I know that that was implemented without a good medical evaluation. If corrections is true to form, they have implemented this [the stun belt] the same way. Show me a refereed study on this thing." [Stun Tech president Dennis] Kaufman responded that an independent, refereed medical study had never been conducted on the REACT belt.

Some correctional officers wonder about the belt's real purpose, Chase Riveland, former assistant secretary of the Wisconsin Department of Corrections and former secretary of the Washington State Department of Corrections, criticized the stun-belted work crews as a "symbolic statement," designed to give the public an illusion of increased safety. "The thing that concerns me most is the public image that is left out there that says this is going to fix something, stop crime and violence. I guess I don't believe that. The question becomes, how far do we go in brutalization?"

In June 1996, Amnesty International asked the U.S. Bureau of Prisons to suspend use of the electroshock belt, citing the possibility of physical danger to inmates and the potential for misuse. The agency has not complied. In 2000, the United Nations Committee Against Torture asked the United States to ban the belt. The United States has not done so.

Viewpoint 5

"We must . . . end the disgraceful and unconstitutional denial of basic health care in California's prisons."

California Must Spend More on Prison Health Care

J. Clark Kelso

J. Clark Kelso is a professor at the University of the Pacific McGeorge Law School and the federal receiver of the California Prison Health Care System. In the following viewpoint, he notes that federal courts have repeatedly ruled that health care in California's prisons is so inadequate as to be inhumane. Kelso argues that in order to reach constitutional standards and to protect the public from diseases incubated in unhealthy prisons, California must spend $8 billion, mostly on new facilities. Though this is expensive, Kelso maintains, it is necessary, and will be cost-effective in the long run.

As you read, consider the following questions:

1. According to the author, which amendment to the U.S. Constitution has health care in California prisons violated?

J. Clark Kelso, "State Must Invest in Prison Health-Care Facilities," sfgate.com, August 28, 2008. Reproduced by permission of the author.

2. How much of the $8 billion Kelso proposes would be spent on new facilities?
3. What is the average life expectancy in California's prisons, according to the author?

Californians have always persevered. Even through tough emotional and economic times, our American values and a persistent sense of hope and humanity in the face of adversity have served as guiding principles. Now, once again, tough budget choices are spawning an emotional, hot-button debate over the following question: Why should the state spend billions of dollars to provide prisoners with access to basic health care when other important priorities also need funding? In answering this question, we must turn to our basic sense of what is right.

Lack of Health Care Is Inhumane

The U.S. Constitution protects every person in this country from cruel and unusual punishment. It is a time-honored value in all civilized and free societies, and yet, after years of litigation, three federal courts have independently found that the state of California consistently violates the U.S. Constitution's Eighth Amendment [which prohibits cruel and unusual punishment] by failing to provide even the most basic medical, mental health and dental care for its prison inmates. California can and must do better.

A free person has the ability to seek care and determine his or her own course of treatment. But an incarcerated person is fully dependent on the state. Denial of access to treatment or medication can seriously aggravate existing conditions and can even be lethal. In fact, the courts found that unnecessary deaths were frequently occurring in California's prisons because of the lack of basic health care.

Even aside from legal or ideological arguments, there is a reason why every law-abiding Californian must demand that the state provide basic health care in our penal institutions: Public health itself is at risk.

The prisons are a veritable Petri dish for the cultivation of diseases, such as drug-resistant tuberculosis. We need to provide health care to reduce the risk of prison-originated epidemics that may, if not appropriately managed, threaten public health.

That said, $8 billion is a great deal of money. But let me assure you that these are one-time construction costs. We are not creating a Cadillac-quality prison health-care system. No one will ever mistake what we are doing for the Mayo Clinic or a Kaiser [Permanente] health plan. In fact, the scope of health-care services that will be available in our prisons under my plan will be similar to the scope of basic services available to every Californian through Medi-Cal or other public medical services programs.

The receiver is seeking a total of $8 billion, rather than the $7 billion originally requested, because the courts have asked the receivership to remedy issues in an additional class-action lawsuit regarding dental care.

Expensive, but Necessary

Of those $8 billion, $6 billion will pay for new facilities, $1 billion will be used to upgrade health-care facilities at the existing 33 correctional facilities, and the new $1 billion will be used to add a dental component to the new facilities and upgrade the existing institutions with dental resources.

That impacts the health and well-being of all 170,000 inmates in one fashion or another.

Yet the cost of delivering basic health care in prison is high. In part, that's because we take our job of protecting the public very seriously. A large portion of our expenses will go toward ensuring the safety and security of our facilities and the communities nearby.

California to Cut Prison Population

A panel of federal judges ordered the California prison system [in August 2009] to reduce its inmate population of 150,000 by 40,000—roughly 27 percent—within two years.

The judges said that reducing prison crowding in California was the only way to change what they called an unconstitutional prison health care system that causes one unnecessary death a week.

In a scathing 184-page order, the judges said state officials had failed to comply with previous orders to fix the prison health care system and reduce crowding.

Solomon Moore, New York Times, *August 4, 2009.*

Also, the prison population has a significantly higher proportion of patients with serious, chronic conditions than the general population. The prison population ages faster than the general population, and the prisoners' health shows it. The average life expectancy in the United States is 75 years; in California's prisons, it's 54. Prisoners have very high incidence of hepatitis, HIV, diabetes, liver disease and other conditions associated with excessive drug use. These are expensive conditions to treat, and almost 60 percent of inmates are on some form of prescription drug.

The simple truth is that we are trying to reduce overall operational costs. Consolidating our 10,000 sickest inmates in the seven health-care facilities I propose to build, allows us to greatly reduce the high costs of transporting sick inmates to far away health-care facilities. It will also be much more cost effective to provide them with medications and treatments in a centralized location.

There is another benefit to the state. The 10,000 beds that the receivership corporation will be building for health care purposes will free up the same number of beds in existing prisons and significantly reduce the overcrowding problem. (With 172,000 inmates in 33 facilities, the state's correctional system is operating at double capacity.) In turn, that should make good rehabilitation and vocational training programs more feasible.

I am committed to bringing California's prison health-care system up to basic and humane constitutional standards in the quickest, most cost-effective manner possible. Beware of the demagogues who are trying to use trick math to convince the public that we are planning to spend lavishly on each prisoner per year. They fail to mention that this one-time capital investment will provide the state with a cost-effective solution for upholding our constitutional responsibilities by providing health care to inmates with chronic conditions for the next 40 or 50 years.

We must turn our prison health-care services around and end the disgraceful and unconstitutional denial of basic health care in California's prisons. We must live by our principles and values of hope and humanity.

> *"[Prisoners] aren't animals, but they aren't entitled to facilities that far exceed those available to the average law-abiding taxpayer."*

California Should Not Spend Excessively on Prison Health Care

Debra Saunders

Debra Saunders is a conservative syndicated columnist. In the following viewpoint, she argues that the plan put forward by court-appointed receiver J. Clark Kelso to upgrade the prison health care system is too lavish and includes unnecessary frills, like gymnasiums. Saunders maintains that California has substantially improved prison health care in the last few years. Given that, and given Califonria's budget crisis, Saunders maintains that Kelso's proposals are extravagant and unnecessary.

As you read, consider the following questions:

1. According to Saunders, what will be the cost per inmate of operating Kelso's new health facilities?
2. According to the author, by how much did inmate deaths fall between 2006 and 2008?

Debra Saunders, "California's Health Care for Inmates: Prison or Versailles?" *National Ledger*, January 31, 2009. By permission of Debra Saunders and Creators Syndicate, Inc.

3. What is the California state budget gap, according to Saunders?

Of course California's prison inmates are entitled to reasonable 21st-century health care. Unfortunately for taxpayers, Clark Kelso, the federal receiver in charge of California's prison health care has, as state Attorney General Jerry Brown noted at a news conference [in January 2009], a "gold-plated wish list" for California's prison health care system.

Pampering Inmates

His Receivership wants to spend $8 billion to build seven new hospitals, each the size of 10 Wal-Marts, which would create "a holistic environment," with "music therapy, art therapy and other recreation therapy functions," a music room, stress-reduction room, game room and "therapy kitchen," with lots of natural light and high ceilings. A gymnasium would feature a "full-size high school playing court with basketball hoops and built-in edge seating up to four rows deep. Various floor striping allows for other games, such as volleyball, etc. Other sport activities include handball courts, exercise, and (a) work-out room."

"The overarching value" of Plan Kelso is to create "a health care facility that cares for prisoners as patients and not a prison that cares for health care needs as inmates." No surprise: The California Department of Corrections and Rehabilitation estimates the annual cost of operating these facilities to be between $170,000 and $230,000 per inmate.

The amazing part: California politicians were going along with the plan until . . . Governor Arnold Schwarzenegger and Brown filed a motion asking U.S. District Court Judge Thelton E. Henderson to replace Kelso with a special master.

Like hell, His Receivership's plans were paved with good intentions. When Henderson stepped in, he wrote in 2005, California's prison medical care system was so broken that "an inmate in one of California's prisons needlessly (died) every six to seven days." Henderson found that in some facilities, hygiene was optional and staffers were substandard. A San Quentin dentist wouldn't even wash his hands or change gloves between patients. I'm tough on crime, but that's criminal and unacceptable.

Henderson's remedies, however, have had their problems, as well. The first receiver, Robert Sillen, once threatened to "back up the Brinks truck" to the state's treasury to bankroll better inmate care—and he clearly meant it. Sillen was paid $775,790 in the 15 months, ending in June 2007. An audit found no fraud, but it found that Sillen authorized $218,790 in overpayments to staff members for such benefits as health insurance and retirement that they already had received.

Henderson fired Sillen and then hired Kelso, who set his own annual salary at $224,000—plus a possible bonus. The Schwarzenegger-Brown motion complains that Kelso's "large staff and $74 million in administrative expenses" are duplicative and amount to a full-scale takeover of the state prison health care system.

Gains Have Been Made

In the meantime, health care spending per inmate rose from $7,601 per inmate in 2005–06 to $13,778 per inmate in 2007–08—an 81 percent increase and far above the average of $4,600 spent on health care per Californian. Kelso boasts of "an influx of new physicians and nurses"—including 172 board-certified physicians, 488 registered nurses and 533 licensed vocational nurses—in part because of big salary increases. The number of inmate deaths has fallen dramatically, from 124 in the first quarter of 2006 to 87 in the second quarter of 2008. The number of "preventable" deaths fell to three in 2007. At the news conference, California's corrections secretary, Matt Cate, credited the receiver for such improvements.

Releasing Prisoners to Balance Budget

The [California] State Senate approved Governor Arnold Schwarzenegger's proposal to trim $1.2 billion from the prison system by releasing 37,000 inmates.

Supported by the majority of the Democratic Caucus, which outnumbers the Republicans by five, the bill would release 27,000 inmates this fiscal year [2009–10] and 10,000 inmates next fiscal year—if passed by the Assembly too. . . .

Democrats said the plan would improve a dysfunctional criminal justice system.

"We return 70 percent of all parolees back to prison," said Senate President Pro Tem Darrell Steinberg. "This is an opportunity to do better and to begin to change the embarrassing fact that we spend more money on prisons than we do the University of California system."

Hoa Quach, SDNN.com, August 20, 2009. www.sdnn.com.

With all those gains, I wondered, doesn't that mean His Receivership can drop the building plans? Kelso thinks not. He told me over the telephone Thursday that he believes the $13,778 number is inflated by the inclusion of correctional officer salaries. Also, he argued that costs for dental and mental health—which he took on to help the Corrections Department—drove up the costs. If he eliminated mental health, he could reduce the up-to-$230,000-per-inmate estimate substantially. And come to think of it, maybe he'll throw mental health back to the state.

While mortality and preventable deaths are down, "possibly preventable deaths" are up. "We're up about 15 to 20 percent through our Turnaround Plan," he said, which suggests his plans are too ambitious.

I think the "holistic" language was a mistake. He countered, "You're right about that." Kelso rightly closed in noting, "These people are not animals"—and doctors should treat them as patients. But his operation is completely out of touch with fiscal realities. As state Finance Director Mike Genest noted, with Schwarzenegger trying to fill a $41.6 billion budget hole, "We're having to cut back everywhere." But Kelso is all plus signs.

And His Receivership doesn't quite understand the population he serves. The yoga/music therapy/handball/landscaping—that's right, I forgot to mention the landscaping to give facilities that retreat feeling—approach fails to recognize that 47 percent of California's inmates are repeat violent offenders.

They aren't animals, but they aren't entitled to facilities that far exceed those available to the average law-abiding taxpayer. As Brown noted, California is spending "almost three times what the federal government is spending, more than two times what the average Californian gets. When is enough enough?"

Periodical Bibliography

The following articles have been selected to supplement the diverse views presented in this chapter.

Michael B. Farrell	"California Assembly Passes Diluted Prison Reform Bill," *Christian Science Monitor*, September 1, 2009.
Niall Green	"Prison Riot in California," World Socialist Web Site, August 13, 2009. www.wsws.org.
Laurence Hammack	"Investigation of Prison Fades Away," *Roanoke (VA) Times*, May 29, 2006.
Eli Lehrer	"Eliminating Prison Rape," *National Review Online*, June 23, 2009. www.nationalreview.com/corner.
Solomon Moore	"The Prison Overcrowding Fix," *New York Times*, February 10, 2009.
National Union of Public and General Employees	"Canada's Federal Prison Guards to Test Stun Guns This Year," January 11, 2007.
New York Times	"Prison Rape," June 23, 2009.
Esteban Parra	"With Poor Health Care Ratings, State's Prisons in Danger of Being Taken Over," *DelawareOnline*, September 30, 2009. www.delawareonline.com.
Sherwood Ross	"Solitary Confinement in U.S. Prisons Making Thousands Psychotic," *LA Progressive*, March 26, 2009.
Sonja Starr	"Solitary Confinement: Possibly Torture, Definitely Hell," *Concurring Opinions*, April 1, 2009. www.concurringopinions.com.
Laura Sullivan	"As Populations Swell, Prisons Rethink Supermax," *NPR Online*, July 27, 2006. www.npr.org.

Chapter 4

How Should Different Prison Populations Be Treated?

Chapter Preface

In some situations, the justice system may try, or be required, to treat specific populations of prisoners in particular ways. One group that is sometimes treated separately is white-collar criminals.

White-collar crimes are crimes generally committed by white-collar workers in the course of their occupations. White-collar crimes include fraud, bribery, insider trading, embezzlement, computer crime, identity theft, and forgery. White-collar crime is usually nonviolent, and its perpetrators are usually relatively well-off and socially respectable.

Because of the nature of the crimes and the status of the perpetrators, white-collar criminals have traditionally been less likely to receive prison time for their offenses. Jack Oceano, a lawyer, explained the rationale in a June 27, 2006, article on the Associated Content Web site. According to Oceano, "Incarcerating white collar criminals does not advance the concept of even-handed justice. On the contrary, it tips the scales and undermines the seriousness of violence. Intermediate and informal sanctions achieve the necessary goals of deterrence and retribution without giving rise to concerns over prison overcrowding, costs, safety and reintegration."

Because of such concerns, traditionally when white-collar inmates have been incarcerated, they have often been placed in less-harsh prison camps. A May 11, 2003, article in *USA Today* by Jayne O'Donnell and Richard Willing notes that in such facilities, offenders "are often housed fewer to a room. Camp inmates can meet with visitors outdoors on the camp grounds, walk around freely on the property and often do more fulfilling work than in low-security prisons."

Not everyone believes that such leniency in white-collar cases is warranted, however. Especially following the massive Enron accounting fraud scandal of 2001, there has been a push to make executives "do much longer sentences in tougher prisons," as the *USA Today* article put it. Howard Gleckman, writing in a January 2, 2002, article in *Business Week*, argued that "Unfortunately, this country has a long and sad history of letting hustlers, stock market manipulators, and other white-collar con artists off the hook." Gleckman maintained that executives who committed fraud should go to prison to "discourage" others from committing similar crimes.

This was also the rationale behind the sentencing of Bernie Madoff, who masterminded one of the largest financial frauds in history, costing investors in funds he managed more than $50 billion. According to Tomoeh Murakami Tse writing in the *Washington Post* on June 30, 2009, the judge in the case, Denny Chin, sentenced Madoff to 150 years in prison because "'the message must be sent that Mr. Madoff's crimes were extraordinarily evil.'" How to send that message, protect the public, and still fairly and humanely address the needs of different prison populations is a question that confronts society when dealing with many groups, whether it be white-collar criminals, juveniles, women, or the mentally ill, as debated in the following viewpoints.

Viewpoint 1

> "A prison may not seem like the best place to raise infants. But researchers are finding that it's better than the alternative."

Allowing Inmate Moms to Raise Their Children in Prison Is Beneficial

Suzanne Smalley

Suzanne Smalley is a national correspondent for Newsweek. *In the following viewpoint, she reports on the growth of nurseries in women's prisons. Smalley notes that infant care in prison has grown in popularity in recent years because more and more women have been incarcerated and because keeping women with their children seems to lower recidivism rates. Experts also argue that keeping infants with their mothers is good for the children, and may reduce the chances of the child ending up in prison later in life.*

As you read, consider the following questions:

1. How many infants does Smalley say were in the nursery at the Indiana prison she visited?

Suzanne Smalley, "Bringing Up Baby in the Big House," *Newsweek*, www.newsweek.com, May 14, 2009.

2. The nursery program is offered only to inmates with how much time remaining on their sentences when they give birth, according to the author?
3. What percentage of prison nursery moms returned to jail, according to Smalley?

The special wing of the Indiana Women's Prison is at once cheerful and depressing. To get there, you walk through a metal detector and a locked steel door to a courtyard surrounded by razor wire and two 20-foot fences. Then you pass through two more steel doors, and eventually enter a cinder-block hallway. The bright yellow hallway is adorned with stenciled images of stars and crescent moons. The sound of a TV blares from a common room, decorated with a mural of the night sky and the lyrics to "Twinkle, Twinkle, Little Star." There are cells on both sides of the hallway. Each has a varnished crib that was made in woodworking class. Protective collars are fitted to the cell doors—there to prevent the steel from slamming on little fingers.

Raising Infants in Prison

A prison may not seem like the best place to raise infants. But researchers are finding that it's better than the alternative. Joseph Carlson, a criminal-justice professor at the University of Nebraska at Kearney who recently completed a 10-year study, says he thought such programs were "strange" when he began his research. Now he thinks they're "a win-win situation" for mothers and babies—and reduce crime by helping inmates to reform. Carlson also believes such programs can help "stop the generational cycle" in which children of inmates become criminals themselves. "Our goal is that the child will feel loved, the mother will stay out of prison herself and thus will hopefully strive to keep the child out of prison," says Carlson, whose study [was] published [in spring 2009] by the journal *Corrections Compendium*.

The nursery at the Indiana prison was opened [in 2008]. Since then, about 20 infants have joined an inmate population of more than 400. There is already a waiting list of four women who qualified for the program but can't get in. If there's not an opening by the time they give birth, they'll have to give up their kids.

Sometimes the mothers in the program attend a class with Angela Tomlin, a clinical psychologist who teaches child-care skills. At a recent session, the women talked about bonding, breast-feeding and singing songs to their infants. They spoke about their own routines and laughed as they shared child-rearing stories. Tomlin explained how to hold a child during feeding so "babies can see you, and you can work on your eye contact."

Better than the Alternative

Jessica Utter, 33, wishes she could have any kind of contact at all with her baby. She is one of four women working in the nursery, helping the mothers and cleaning the rooms for $1.30 a day. Like many of the inmates at Indiana Women's Prison, Utter has been in and out of jail for years. She gave birth to her eighth child on the day after Christmas in 2007, shortly after arriving at the prison on charges of peddling cocaine. But facing a long sentence as a repeat offender, Utter couldn't keep her baby. The nursery program is offered only to inmates with 18 months or less remaining on their sentences when they give birth. "You just leave your baby in the hospital within 24 hours," says Utter, a fast-talking Midwesterner who won't be free again until 2014 (at the earliest). She began to cry as she explained that she'll soon see her youngest child for the first time since she was born. Utter's parents, who take care of the infant and two of her other children, live in Wisconsin and couldn't afford to travel to Indiana for visiting day; a church donated the few hundred dollars required for their bus fare.

Indiana Women Prisoner Boom

The number of women in Indiana prisons has risen 61 percent from 2000 to 2008, which is more than twice the national rate and significantly higher than the rate of Hoosier [residents of Indiana] men.

Precisely why this is happening is not clear, but experts cite several factors. Mandatory drug sentencing laws, a bad economy and a rising tide of prescription drug and methamphetamine arrests are among them.

Lurking behind the statistics, however, experts also see a broader societal change.

"The gloves have been taken off," said Natalie Sokoloff, a sociology professor at New York's John Jay College of Criminal Justice who has written books on female incarceration. "Some criminal justice people say, 'OK, women want equality; we'll give them equality.'"

Francesca Jarosz, Indystar.com, July 21, 2009. www.indystar.com.

Prison nurseries didn't spread in earnest until recently. New York state opened the country's first in 1902, but it was the exception until 1994, when Nebraska followed suit. Since the late '90s, seven new prison nurseries have opened, including four that have opened (or been approved to open) in the past two years [2007–08]. Now Texas and Kansas are reportedly mulling similar programs. Part of the reason: the rate of female incarceration has exploded nationwide—growing more than eightfold since the mid-'70s—and prison administrators are looking for effective ways to reduce recidivism. The Nebraska study compared the records of 65 mothers who participated in a prison nursery with a control group of 30 pregnant inmates who had their babies taken away within 72 hours of birth. Only 17 percent of the prison nursery moms returned to jail, while 50 percent of the control group did. It costs as little as $13 a day per baby to run a prison nursery. By comparison, the per-inmate cost of running a prison is closer to $75 a day.

Many prison moms didn't have much of an upbringing themselves. Devan Toomer, who is serving three and a half years for shoplifting, has been living in the Indiana prison nursery since it opened. Sentenced as a habitual offender, Toomer said she used to support her family by stealing and reselling clothes at half price. Her son, Devion, is now 1. But Toomer also has a 4-year-old daughter who is living with Toomer's mother. That may seem like a good alternative, but Toomer says her relationship with her mother has sometimes been strained, and she was raised largely by a family friend. (Toomer's mother could not be located for comment.)

Some prison guards aren't sympathetic toward the women. They make snide remarks that children don't belong in jail. That attitude angers Toomer, who admits to loving "fast money" but wants to get a college degree when she gets out. "I don't look at it as the babies doing time," she says, "because all the baby knows is they're with their mother and that's where children prefer to be."

VIEWPOINT 2

> *"Many countries haven't figured out how to punish the mother, honor the importance of keeping babies or young children with their mothers, and simultaneously not punish the child."*

Raising Children in Prison May Be Harmful

Carol Lloyd

Carol Lloyd is a writer, performer, and entrepreneur whose work has appeared in publications such as the New York Times Magazine, San Francisco Examiner, *and* Salon. *In the following viewpoint, she notes that in many nations, including the United States, an effort is made to allow mothers to keep their children while in prison. Lloyd acknowledges the importance of keeping children with their mothers but believes that kids living in prison may suffer abuse and deprivation.*

As you read, consider the following questions:

1. As the author reports, until what age do children in Mexico stay with their mothers in prison?

Carol Lloyd, "When Mom's In Prison, Should Her Baby Be Behind Bars Too?" *Salon*, February 7, 2008. This article first appeared in Salon.com, at http://www.salon.com. An online version remains in the Salon archives. Reprinted with permission.

2. According to Lloyd, until what developmental stage are children in the United States allowed to stay with their mothers in prison?

3. According to the report the author cites, are there extensive specific international standards regarding the treatment of children in prison with their mothers?

A story in the *Chicago Tribune* explores a bizarre policy adopted by Mexico City concerning children in prison. Since the 1990s, children born to incarcerated women inside the city's prisons are required to stay with their mothers until the age of 6. It's not an option; it's a requirement. The government applies the law with irrational consistency—the kids stay with Mom even when there's a history of violence. In one instance mentioned in the article, a woman who had been convicted of causing her stepson's death was allowed to keep her baby.

Disturbing Images

The article is filled with disturbing images: a brightly colored preschool behind bars, children living with their mothers along with two other mothers and their children in a 144-square-foot cell, children getting frequent respiratory illnesses from the damp, drafty cells, kids spending afternoons after school walking the exercise yard. Everyone—both staff and incarcerated alike—emphasizes the positive influence of the children on the mothers and the relative safety of these children surrounded by a "collective maternal instinct." But for me, the most heartbreaking part of the law is not so much tots doing time behind bars but the fact that, at 6 years old, the children—who have been more dependent on their mothers than most children out in society might have been—are suddenly taken away from the one person they know best.

The U.S. Women Prison Population, 2000–2008

Year	Women Prisoners
2000	92,234
2001	92,979
2002	97,631
2003	100,846
2004	104,822
2005	107,626
2006	112,459
2007	114,407
2008	115,779

TAKEN FROM: Heather C. West and William J. Sabol, "Prison Inmates at Midyear, 2008 Statistical Tables," Bureau of Justice Statistics, April 8, 2009. www.ojp.usdoj.gov.

The Mexican government has obviously made a policy decision based on the idea that early-childhood bonding with a mother trumps most other concerns. And though studies do show that it's good for kids with parents in prison to spend time with them, isn't this a little wacko?

When reading this story, I assumed this was an anomalous practice, rare in the rest of the world. But according to a policy paper, "Violence Against Babies and Small Children Living in Prison With Their Mothers" by the Quaker United Nations Office, many countries allow similar arrangements, though policies vary widely in upper age limits. Policies also vary in how the prison defines the arrangement—some maintain that living with children is a privilege, others that it's a right. (I didn't find other countries or municipalities that make it a requirement.) How well the prisons accommodate the presence of innocent inmates also varies, from European countries taking great pains to make sure the children don't know they are in prison to children being warehoused in huge dormitories with their mothers and other inmates.

No Good Solutions

Countries as diverse as Cambodia, Bolivia, Pakistan and Spain allow children to live in prison up to the age of 6. Some countries make different decisions based on the kind of prison—in Germany children may live in closed prisons only until 3 but in open prisons (with lower security) until 6. France, Malta, the United Kingdom, Finland and the U.S. allow children to live behind bars until they are toddlers. Others, like New Zealand, Iceland, Ghana, Hungary and Ireland, only allow babies to live in the big house and in some cases only while the mother is breast-feeding. Mexico seems to occupy the edge of the spectrum with children of any age permitted to stay with their mother.

What's clear from the report (which chronicles lots of egregious abuse by fellow inmates and staff, institutional neglect and lack of government oversight for the children) is that many countries haven't figured out how to punish the mother, honor the importance of keeping babies or young children with their mothers, and simultaneously not punish the child. "Whilst there is a wealth of international law and guidelines concerning imprisonment, there are almost no specific standards regarding the treatment of children in prison with their mothers," the report concludes. "With few exceptions, states and the United Nations human rights mechanisms have given little consideration to the rights and needs of children in prison with their mothers."

I'm torn. Anytime a mother gets imprisoned it's obviously a lose-lose-lose situation for mother, baby and society at large. But is the answer curtailing kids' freedom to keep them under a mother's wing? Or is this just another way humanity has learned to throw the baby out with the bathwater?

Viewpoint 3

> *"Jail staff are simply not equipped to protect youth from the dangers of adult jails."*

Juveniles Should Not Be Placed in Adult Prisons

Campaign for Youth Justice

The Campaign for Youth Justice (CFYJ) is an organization dedicated to ending the practice of trying, sentencing, and incarcerating youth under age eighteen in the adult criminal justice system. In the following viewpoint, CFYJ argues that juveniles who serve time in adult prison are at increased risk of suicide, at increased risk of sexual assault, and more likely to reoffend. CFYJ also argues that adult prisons are not equipped to handle juveniles' educational and developmental needs.

As you read, consider the following questions:

1. About how many juveniles does CFYJ assert are incarcerated in U.S. adult jails?
2. How many times more likely is a juvenile to commit suicide if he or she is in an adult jail, according to the author?

Campaign for Youth Justice, *Jailing Juveniles: The Dangers of Incarcerating Youth In Adult Jails in America*, November, 2007. Reproduced by permission.

3. According to CFYJ, what percentage of adult jails provide no educational services at all?

Every day in America, an average of 7,500 youth are incarcerated in adult jails. The annual number of youth who are placed in adult jails is even higher—ten or twenty times the daily average according to some researchers—to account for the "turnover rate" of youth entering and exiting adult jails. Despite the life-altering consequences of incarceration in an adult jail, relatively little attention has been given to these youth. This report presents the latest research about the risks youth face in jail, the number and characteristics of youth incarcerated in jails across the country, the lack of state and federal laws protecting youth in jails, and concludes with recommendations for federal, state, and county policymakers.

Youth at Risk in Adult Jails

It is extremely difficult to keep youth safe in adult jails. When youth are placed with adults in jails, youth are at great risk of physical and sexual assault. For example, according to U.S. Department of Justice Bureau of Justice Statistics (BJS) in 2005 and 2006, 21% and 13%, respectively, of the victims of inmate-on-inmate sexual violence in jails were youth under the age of 18—a surprisingly high percentage of victims considering that only 1% of all jail inmates are juveniles.

Recognizing the risks to youth in jails, some jailers separate youth from adult inmates. However, this is not an adequate solution either. Separating youth from adults in jail can reduce the physical or emotional harm that may result from contact with adult offenders, but unfortunately these youth are then often placed in isolation, a dangerous setting for youth. Youth in isolation are frequently locked down 23 hours a day in small cells with no natural light. Even limited exposure to such an environment can cause anxiety, paranoia, exacerbate existing mental disorders, and increase risk of suicide. In fact, youth have the highest suicide rates of all inmates in jails. Youth are 19 times more likely to commit suicide in jail than youth in the general population and 36 times more likely to commit suicide in an adult jail than in a juvenile detention facility. Jail staff are simply not equipped to protect youth from the dangers of adult jails.

Jails do not have the capacity to provide the necessary education and other programs crucial for the healthy development of adolescents. Even though legally required to, few jails provide appropriate education to youth. A BJS survey found that 40% of jails provided no educational services at all, only 11% of jails provided special education services, and only 7% provided vocational training. As many as one-half of all youth transferred to the adult system do not receive adult convictions, and are returned to the juvenile justice system or are not convicted at all. Many of these youth will have spent *at least one month* in an adult jail and one in five of these youth will have spent *over six months* in an adult jail. Without adequate education and other services, jails take youth off course.

More Likely to Reoffend

Research conducted nationally by the MacArthur Foundation Research Network on Adolescent Development and Juvenile Justice, and other organizations, has also found that placing youth in the adult criminal justice system increases their likelihood of re-offending. Physicians and criminologists agree that children who are prosecuted in adult court are more likely to be re-arrested more often and more quickly for serious offenses. The Centers for Disease Control and Prevention Task Force on Community Preventive Services released findings that show that transferring youth to the adult criminal system increases violence and concluded that policies that send youth to the adult criminal justice system, including placement of youth in adult jails, are "counterproductive for the purpose of reducing violence and enhancing public safety."

Dangers of Prison Rape

During a hearing on the Prison Rape Reduction Act in July 2002, a former state attorney general testified that "anywhere from 250,000 to 600,000" prisoners were forced to have sex against their will each year. The result is an HIV infection rate of at least 8.5 percent in New York state's correctional system. . . .

Judging by my 18 years of penitentiary experience, those 250,000 to 600,000 inmate rape victims include nearly all juveniles . . . who are sent to adult facilities.

Jens Soering,
National Catholic Reporter,
November 19, 2004.

Finally, the federal Juvenile Justice & Delinquency Prevention Act (JJDPA) enacted over three decades ago was designed to keep youth out of jails. However, there is a loophole—the law does not protect youth prosecuted in the adult criminal system even though the original intent of the federal law was to remove youth from adult jails altogether. Congress should fix this problem by amending the JJDPA to protect all youth, no matter what court (juvenile or criminal) they are in, from being placed in an adult jail. Similarly, states and counties should update their state statutes and policies to prohibit the placement of youth in adult jails. . . .

Radically Different Services

State and federal laws should acknowledge the developmental stage of adolescence by banning the incarceration of youth in adult jails. Adult jails are designed to house adults, whereas juvenile detention facilities are designed for youth. The result is that juvenile and adult detention facilities provide radically different services for the people in their facilities. From intake processes to meals to health care, adolescents have specific needs that jails are often ill-equipped to handle. For example, youth have different nutritional requirements because they are growing so rapidly. Vision and dental health are two additional areas that change during adolescence and require special attention. If youth do not receive appropriate physical and mental health care, their development can be compromised forever.

One main reason why juvenile detention facilities are better suited for adolescents is staffing. Jail staff who supervise youth are often put in awkward and dangerous positions because the "right way" to handle 99% of the inmates in their facilities (the adults) is usually the "wrong way" for the remaining 1% (developing youth who happen to be inmates). Juvenile detention facilities generally operate with higher levels of staffing (one staff person to eight youth) compared to jails (ratios can be as high as one staff person to 64 inmates). Youth themselves report important differences between staff at juvenile facilities and those at adult facilities. Researchers have found that youth in juvenile facilities rated staff as being more helpful in assisting them with meeting their personal goals, teaching them skills, and improving their interpersonal relations, compared with youth in adult facilities. Additional staffing is critical for engaging youth in exercise, education, and pro-social activities necessary for proper development. Juvenile detention facilities also find it easier to offer these activities because they usually have access to dayrooms, classroom space, or gyms, and are not as constrained by the physical limitations of many jails. Many jails are unable to offer these programs because youth need to be kept safe from the other adult inmates, and as a result are kept within cells or sections of jails.

The lack of education programs in jails has particularly serious consequences for youth who can be detained for several months pre-trial. Because of their age, most youth in jails have not completed their high school education and need classes to graduate or obtain a GED [general education development, high school equivalency degree], or to acquire vocational skills to get a job. Without adequate schooling, too many youth are at risk of falling further and further behind academically even though they are legally entitled to an education. Most states have mandatory attendance laws requiring that children attend school unless they have obtained a diploma or a GED. The federal special education law, Individuals with Disabilities Education Act (IDEA), also requires jails to provide special education services for qualifying youth; however, jails frequently have difficulty meeting their legal obligations. For example, at the Madison Street Maricopa County Jail in Arizona, education programs were limited to three hours per day and did not provide an option for obtaining a diploma. The Orange County Grand Jury in California, a citizen oversight commission, found that "the opportunity for rehabilitation and education of juveniles is extremely difficult because there is neither adequate classroom space nor opportunity for minimum classroom instruction time at Central Men's Jail." While juvenile detention centers often have full-time education staff, adult jails have weak educational programs and it is rare for jails to have classrooms for education. Although nearly 30% of jail inmates under age 24 reported having a learning disability, the most recent survey of educational programs in adult jails found that 40% of jails provided no educational services at all, only 11% provided special education services, and just 7% provided vocational training.

Viewpoint 4

> *"Life without parole for the very worst juvenile offenders is reasonable."*

Life Without Parole in the Adult System Is Reasonable for Some Juvenile Offenders

Charles D. Stimson and Andrew M. Grossman

Charles D. Stimson is a senior legal fellow at the Heritage Foundation, a military trial judge, and a former prosecutor. Andrew M. Grossman has served as a senior legal policy analyst at the Heritage Foundation. In the following viewpoint, they argue that trying juveniles as adults and sentencing them to life without parole for particularly heinous crimes is reasonable. The authors argue that there is a serious problem with juvenile crime in the United States and maintain that neither the Constitution nor international treaties prevent the United States from implementing life without parole for juveniles.

As you read, consider the following questions:

1. What do the authors call the statistic showing that there are 2,225 juveniles serving life-without-parole sentences in the United States?

Charles D. Stimson and Andrew M. Grossman, "Adult Time for Adult Crimes: Life Without Parole for Juvenile Killers and Violent Teens," The Heritage Foundation, August, 2009. Reproduced by permission.

2. Where does the United States rank in murders committed by youth per capita, according to Stimson and Grossman?
3. According to the authors, why does the Convention on the Rights of the Child not apply in the United States?

Life without parole [LWOP] for the very worst juvenile offenders is reasonable, constitutional, and (appropriately) rare. In response to the Western world's worst juvenile crime problem, U.S. legislators have enacted commonsense measures to protect their citizens and hold these dangerous criminals accountable. Forty-three states, the District of Columbia, and the federal government have set the maximum punishment for juvenile offenders at life without the possibility of parole. By the numbers, support for its use is overwhelming.

Life Without Parole at Risk

Nonetheless, its continued viability is at risk from misleading lobbying efforts in many states and court cases that seek to substitute international law for legislative judgments and constitutional text.

Emboldened by the Supreme Court's [2005] *Roper v. Simmons* decision, which relied on the Eighth Amendment's "cruel and unusual punishments" language to prohibit capital sentences for juveniles, anti-incarceration activists have set about extending the result of *Roper* to life without parole. If they succeed, an important tool of criminal punishment will be eliminated, and all criminal sentences could be subjected to second-guessing by judges, just as they are in capital punishment cases today.

The most visible aspects of this campaign are a number of self-published reports and "studies" featuring photographs of young children and litigation attacking the constitutionality of life without parole for juvenile offenders—including two cases that the U.S. Supreme Court has agreed to hear in its 2009 term.

Because the activists have monopolized the debate over life without parole, legislatures, courts, the media, and the public have been misled on crucial points. For example, dozens of newspaper articles, television reports, and court briefs have echoed the activists' assertion that 2,225 juvenile offenders are serving LWOP sentences in the United States, despite that this figure is nothing more than a manufactured statistic....

Necessary and Constitutional

Activists argue that the United States does not need life-without-parole sentences for juvenile offenders because other Western nations, particularly in Europe, do not use it. In fact, the need is real.

In one recent year, juveniles committed as many violent crimes in the United States as in the next seven highest countries combined. The U.S. ranks third in murders committed by youths and 14th in murders per capita committed by youths, putting it in the same league as Panama, the Philippines, Kazakhstan, Paraguay, Cuba, and Belarus.

Also contrary to activists' arguments, the Constitution does not forbid use of the sentence. The Eighth Amendment's prohibition on "cruel and unusual punishments" was intended to bar only the most "inhuman and barbarous" punishments, like torture. Though the Supreme Court has departed from this original meaning, it has honored the principle that courts should defer to lawmakers in setting sentences in almost every instance.

One exception applies to punishments that are "grossly disproportionate to the crime," something that the Court has found only in a handful of cases. Otherwise, the Court has approved harsh punishments for a variety of offenses so long

Most States Allow Life Sentences Without Parole for Juveniles

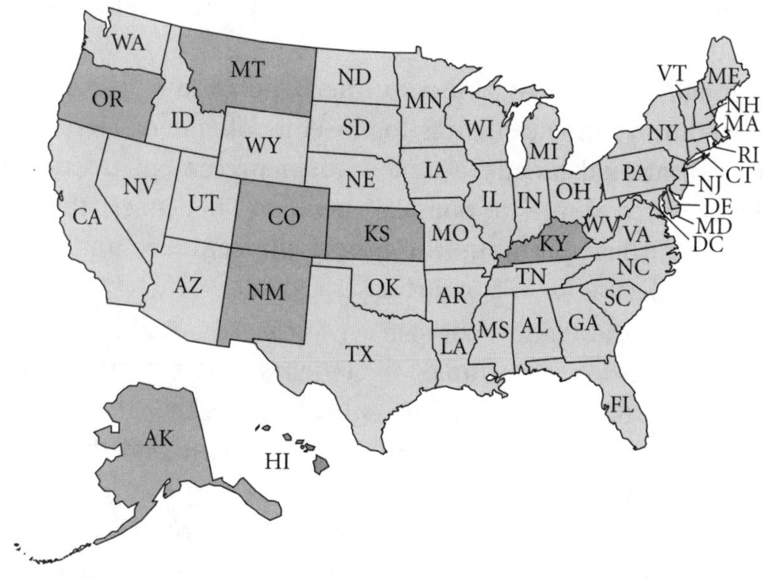

States with statutes allowing life sentences without parole for juvenile offenders

States that do not allow life sentences without parole for juvenile offenders

TAKEN FROM: Charles D. Stimson and Andrew M. Grossman, "Adult Time for Adult Crimes: Life Without Parole for Juvenile Killers and Violent Teens," Heritage Foundation Web Site, August 2009, www.heritage.org.

as legislatures have a "reasonable basis" for believing that the punishment advances the criminal-justice system's goals. Because no state imposes life without parole for minor crimes, the punishment will never be constitutionally disproportionate. The other exception applies only in death-penalty cases like *Roper*, and the Court has long refused to subject non-death punishments to the deep scrutiny that it uses in capital cases.

Even ignoring that distinction, the argument that *Roper* could be extended to life-without-parole sentences comes up short. Indeed, the *Roper* Court actually relied on the availability of the sentence to justify prohibiting the juvenile death penalty.

Finally, the activists turn to international law to challenge life-without-parole sentences for juvenile offenders, relying on the aspirational language that is often present in treaties to advance their domestic political agendas. They assert that international law prohibits the use of the sentence and is directly applicable in U.S. court cases.

In this, they ignore almost every rule about the relationship between international agreements and U.S. law. Most treaties are not "self-executing," which means that they can be enforced in domestic courts only to the extent that they have been implemented by statutes.

This variety of treaty, which includes almost every human rights agreement, simply cannot preempt federal or state law acting on its own.

International Treaties Do Not Apply

Treaties do not reach even that point until they have been ratified, as required by the Constitution. Yet activists cite the Convention on the Rights of the Child [CRC], which the United States has not ratified. To get around this, they claim that the CRC has become customary international law. But, like treaties, customary law cannot be enforced in domestic courts until it has been implemented by legislation.

They also give short shrift to reservations that the United States entered when it ratified two other treaties, the International Covenant on Civil and Political Rights and the Convention Against Torture. In both cases, the United States acted to preserve its sovereignty with respect to criminal punishment, limiting the treaties' reach to punishments already forbidden by the Eighth Amendment.

Most juvenile offenders should not and do not have their cases adjudicated in the adult criminal justice system. Every state has a juvenile justice system, and those courts handle the majority of crimes committed by juveniles. But some crimes evince characteristics that push them beyond the leniency otherwise afforded to juveniles: cruelty, wantonness, a complete disregard for the lives of others. Some of these offenders are tried as adults, and a small proportion of them are sentenced to life without parole—the strongest sentence available to express society's disapproval, incapacitate the criminal, and deter the most serious offenses.

A fair look at the Constitution provides no basis for overruling the democratic processes of 43 states, the District of Columbia, and the U.S. Congress. Neither do international law or the misleading and sometimes just wrong statistics and stories marshaled in activists' studies. Used sparingly, as it is, life without parole is an effective and lawful sentence for the worst juvenile offenders. On the merits, it has a place in our laws.

VIEWPOINT 5

"U.S. prisons are not designed or equipped for mentally ill prisoners."

The Mentally Ill Should Not Be Placed in the Prison System

Jamie Fellner

Jamie Fellner is a senior counsel with Human Rights Watch. In the following viewpoint, she argues that the growing number of mentally ill prisoners is straining the prison system. She notes that prisons do not have staff trained to evaluate the mentally ill and provide them with medication and treatment. She also argues that the mentally ill often are unable to follow prison rules, but that prison guards are not trained to take account of this fact, with the result that prisoners often end up being disciplined for actions they cannot control.

As you read, consider the following questions:

1. According to Fellner, how many mentally ill prisoners are there in U.S. jails and prisons?

2. According to the author, apart from mental health services, what special allowances are typically made for prisoners with mental illness?
3. According to Fellner, prisoners have been punished for self-mutilation because the behavior entailed the destruction of what?

The number of incarcerated men and women with severe mental illness has grown so tremendously in the last few decades that prisons may now be the largest mental health providers in the United States. Yet U.S. prisons are not designed or equipped for mentally ill prisoners. Prison conditions are hard on mental health in general, because of overcrowding, violence, lack of privacy, lack of meaningful activities, isolation from family and friends, uncertainty about life after prison, and inadequate health services. The impact of these problems is worse for prisoners whose thinking and emotional responses are impaired by schizophrenia, bipolar disease, major depression, and other serious mental illnesses. The mentally ill in prison also face inadequate mental health services that leave them under-treated or mistreated. In addition, poor mental health services leave many prisoners receiving . . . inappropriate kinds or amounts of psychotropic medication that further impairs their ability to function.

There is an inherent tension between the security mission of prisons and mental health considerations. The formal and informal rules and codes of conduct in prison reflect staff concerns about security, safety, power, and control. Coordinating the needs of the mentally ill with those rules and goals is nearly impossible. . . .

Growing Numbers

There are more than 200,000—perhaps as many as 300,000—men and women in U.S. jails and prisons suffering from mental disorders, including such serious illnesses as schizophrenia, bipolar disorder, and major depression. The proportion of prisoners with mental illness is increasing. The high number and growing proportion of persons with mental illness in U.S. prisons are unintended and tragic consequences of inadequate community mental health services combined with punitive criminal justice policies.

Numerous studies and surveys have documented this rise in the incarceration of the mentally ill. The Bureau of Justice Statistics estimates that sixteen percent of adult inmates in state prisons and local jails are mentally ill. There are three times as many mentally ill people in prisons than in mental health hospitals, and the rate of mental illness in prisons is two to four times greater than in the general public.

Although there is little historical data, corrections and mental health experts believe the proportion of the prison population with mental illness is increasing. Nineteen of thirty-one states responding to a 1998 survey reported a disproportionate increase in their seriously mentally ill population during the previous five years. While some portion of the increase may be attributable to improved mental health screening and diagnosis of mental health problems, there is a consensus in corrections that the numbers also reflect a real change in the rate at which the mentally ill are being sent to prison. . . .

The sheer number of mentally ill inmates has transformed prisons into facilities for the mentally ill. Yet prisons cannot provide the range of services mentally ill prisoners need in the necessary quantity and quality. Seriously ill prisoners confront a paucity of qualified staff to evaluate their illness, develop and implement treatment plans, and monitor their condition. They confront treatment that often consists of little more than medication—and even that may be poorly administered and supervised . . .—or no treatment at all. They live without the diversity of mental health interventions they need, much less the long-term supportive and therapeutic environment that would best help many of them manage their illnesses. Without necessary care, mentally ill inmates suffer painful symptoms and their conditions can deteriorate.

Mentally Ill Prisoners Face Challenges

Apart from the mental health services that may or may not be provided, prisons typically treat prisoners with mental illness identically to all other inmates. There are no special allowances. Officials confine them in the same facilities, expect them to follow the same routines, and require them to comply with the same rules.

Mentally ill prisoners, however, do not have the same capacity to comply with prison rules as do other prisoners. If they have schizophrenia or . . . psychotic symptoms, or other serious dysfunction, inmates may suffer from delusions (false beliefs), hallucinations (erroneous perceptions of reality), chaotic thinking, or serious disruptions of consciousness, memory, and perception of the environment. They may experience debilitating fears or extreme and uncontrollable mood swings. As a result of their illness, they may huddle silently in their cells, mumble incoherently, or yell incessantly. They may hear voices or "command hallucinations," telling them to commit violence against themselves or others. They may exhibit their illness through disruptive behavior, belligerence, aggression, and violence. They may suddenly refuse to follow routine orders, such as to come out of a cell, to stand up for the count, to remove clothes from cell bars, or to take showers. They may beat their heads against cell walls, smear themselves with feces, self-mutilate, and attempt suicide (sometimes succeeding). In short, they may—and often do—behave in ways that prison systems consider punishable misconduct.

The predominant goal of prison authorities is ensuring the security and safety of staff and inmates. This goal is in constant tension with the vulnerabilities of prisoners who have mental illnesses. Prisons operate according to a compre-

Mental Health Courts

The Council of State Governments Justice Center contracted with the RAND Corporation to conduct a fiscal impact study of the Allegheny County Mental Health Court (MHC). The MHC is . . . designed to divert individuals with mental illness who have committed nonviolent crimes from the criminal justice to the mental health treatment system, while preserving public safety. Using administrative data . . . the fiscal impact study identified the treatment, criminal justice, and cash assistance costs for the MHC participants, compared those costs with the costs of routine adjudication and processing, and calculated the fiscal impact of the MHC program.

The findings from our fiscal impact analyses show that entry into the MHC program leads to an increase in the use of mental treatment services in the first year after MHC entry, as well as a decrease in jail time for MHC participants. The decrease in jail expenditures mostly offsets the cost of the treatment services.

However, an analysis that followed a subsample of MHC participants for a longer period of time showed a dramatic decrease in jail costs in the second year of MHC participation. . . . The drop in jail costs more than offset the treatment costs, suggesting that the MHC program may help decrease total taxpayer costs over time.

M. Susan Ridgely et al.,
Justice, Treatment, and Cost, *2007. www.rand.org.*

hensive and complex system of rules, policies, and procedures that regulate all aspects of inmate conduct. Compliance with those rules is paramount. Few accommodations, however, are made for prisoners whose mental illness may make it more likely they will break the rules. While some prison systems have begun to incorporate mental health considerations into their disciplinary systems, there is an urgent and serious need to reassess disciplinary systems in light of rising rates of mentally ill prisoners.

Like other prisoners, those with mental illness navigate the prison environment as best they can, but their illness may leave them less able to conform to the rules. Available data indicate that mentally ill prisoners have higher than average disciplinary rates. . . .

Prison rules operate somewhat like the penal code in the criminal justice system, and the uniformed correctional officers (guards) function in many ways like police, trying to maintain order and charging inmates with "infractions" when they break the rules. The officers have great discretion in deciding which rule violations to write up in a formal "ticket" and how to characterize the nature of the misconduct.

Guards Not Trained

Most prison systems do not provide correctional officers with more than minimal mental health training. Officers typically do not understand the nature of mental illness and its behavioral impact. They cannot distinguish—and may not even know a distinction exists—between a frustrated or disgruntled inmate who "acts out" and one whose "acting out" reflects mental illness. They assume misconduct is volitional or manipulative. When, for example, an officer gives a ticket to an inmate for banging his head against his cell wall, the officer may have little idea that the inmate is experiencing severe uncontrolled hallucinations. As the medical director of one prison system has pointed out, correctional officers all too often "refer prisoners to the disciplinary process even when the prisoners might be having behavioral problems that are a symptom of their illness."

Examples of prisoners accused of breaking rules and being punished for acts connected to mental illness are legion. Prisoners have been punished for self-mutilation because that behavior entailed the "destruction of state property"—to wit, the prisoner's body. Prisoners who tear up bed-sheets to make a rope for hanging themselves have been punished for misusing state property. Prisoners who scream and kick cell doors while hearing voices have been charged with destruction of property and creating a disturbance. And prisoners who smear feces in their cells have been punished for "being untidy." The findings of a federal court examining the treatment of the mentally ill in California prisons are applicable to many other state prison systems:

> Mentally ill inmates who act out are typically treated with punitive measures without regard to their mental status.... There is substantial evidence in the record of seriously mentally ill inmates being treated with punitive measures by the custody staff to control the inmates' behavior without regard to the cause of the behavior, the efficacy of such measures, or the impact of those measures on the inmates' mental illnesses.

VIEWPOINT 6

> *"If prisoners need [mental health] treatment, it is, in large part, for injuries from the institutional violence to which they are subjected in prison."*

Focusing on Mental Illness in Prisons Prevents Real Reform

Susan Mortimer

Susan Mortimer is a prison activist whose disabled brother is a Massachusetts prisoner. In the following viewpoint, she argues that the inhumane conditions of imprisonment, not mental illness, cause prison suicide. Mortimer maintains that more mental health facilities in prison will simply give prison authorities more ways to control, regulate, and dehumanize prisoners. She argues that labeling despairing prisoners as "mentally ill" is simply a way to deny the brutality of prison and to prevent real reform.

As you read, consider the following questions:

1. According to Mortimer, what newspaper has been pushing for ill-conceived prison reforms?
2. What does HB1313 call for, as the author reports?

Susan Mortimer, "Prison Suicide," Massachusetts Statewide Harm Reduction Coalition, April 2008. Reproduced by permission of the author.

3. According to Mortimer, what are Custom Therapeutic Modules (CTMs)?

The rate of 'suicide' in Massachusetts prisons is three times the national rate. In the past two years [2006–07] deaths behind bars have escalated and much attention has been paid to this continuing trend. Ignoring the root causes of such deaths, the Commonwealth and the press (*The Boston Globe*) have pushed instead for ill-conceived reforms, which will increase the suffering of Massachusetts prisoners, but not the safety.

Inhumane Conditions Cause Suicide

Massachusetts Correctional Legal Services, some legislators and the Disability Law Center presume that these deaths were in fact suicide and not murder by the DOC [Department of Corrections]; that the prisoners were 'mentally ill' at the time of their conviction; and that only 'mentally ill' people commit suicide. While we do not have space here to enumerate all the reasons why such presumptions are fallacious, we must acknowledge that racism, poverty and the War on Drugs are the foundation of the prison industrial complex. Powerlessness, constant stress, solitary confinement and sensory deprivation inflict great suffering. Lack of fresh air and exercise, medical neglect and abuse, inadequate nutrition, guard violence, daily deprivation and degradation combine to destroy physical and psychological health. From the extremes of sensory deprivation to seemingly mundane daily occurrences, prison policy and practice violate human rights. Thus, we believe that conditions of confinement, inflicted by the state, manufacture disability.

While we recognize that some behaviors may be viewed as mental illness, designating and placing the focus of an investigation into the deaths of 'mentally ill' prisoners allows administrators, guards and medical staff to evade responsibility for the cruel, inhumane and degrading conditions that engender such desperate behavior. Further, labeling people as 'mentally ill' masks disablement caused by child abuse, poverty, racism, sexism and the coup de grace of prison conditions. Coping responses to inequality and unsafe conditions must be differentiated from 'mental illness'. Counterproductive measures meted out for such coping mechanisms punish individuals for the harms the DOC inflicts upon them. This institutional abuse brings some prisoners to a terrible choice: to live in unending despair or to end their suffering.

The role of paternalism in the development of Residential Treatment Units [live-in health care facilities for the mentally ill] is clear. Liberal reformers want to do the charitable thing. But charity emanates from pity of the allegedly inferior individual; it does not seek to ally with prisoners to work for systemic change. Paternalism originates in privilege and assumed superiority. It is loath to challenge the power of the state. It wants to do what it believes is best for the victim without consulting her. Criminal justice policy born of charitable ideology has had devastating effects on the minds and bodies of incarcerated people. (Quakers advocated penitentiaries as a charitable way to improve prisoners' minds. Prosecutors and jailors use reforms such as parole to punish and to lengthen sentences.)

Enter Massachusetts Correctional Legal Services [MCLS], Representative (and psychologist) Ruth Balser, the Disability Law Center and the *Boston Globe*. The lawyers are suing for Residential Treatment Units (RTU) and Balser is sponsoring HB1313, a bill calling for $40 million for secure mental health units within prisons to be staffed with Department of Mental Health [DMH] employees. *The Globe* has editorialized in favor of RTUs. Last May [2007] during oversight hearings on Prison Suicide and Prison Mental Health at the State House, *Boston Globe* reporter Beth Healy declined to accept written testimony from the only invited group opposed to the treatment units (the Statewide Harm Reduction Coalition). Healy is a member of the Spotlight Team that spent several months working on a three-part investigative series on prison suicides. The exposé is biased toward Residential Treatment Units. It appears to have been directed, particularly regarding the pro-RTU viewpoint, by MCLS' Leslie Walker. Walker is a long-time proponent of RTUs. *The Globe* published her op-ed, touting treatment units, on February 2, 2008. She has ignored prisoners and families who understand that the DOC co-opts reform measures to inflict punishment and to add to its bloated budget.

Prisons Create Despair

By insisting on labeling prisoners who may be suicidal as 'mentally ill', liberal reformers are choosing not to address the root causes of prison deaths. Closer monitoring of suicidal prisoners in RTUs would not treat despair—a product of prison environs. Instead it formalizes policy, protects the DOC administration and consolidates more power in the prison industrial complex.

HB1313 gives wide latitude to DOC superintendents and Commissioner Harold Clarke to administer RTUs under DMH supervision. At present, however, even low-level guards challenge medical orders, withhold pink slips (requests for medical attention), look through patient records and hamper prisoner efforts to get medications in a timely manner. HB1313 does not address guard interference in provision of therapeutic services or guard-on-prisoner violence except to mandate forty hours of mental health training annually for correctional staff assigned to the treatment units. All other guards would be required to undergo eight hours of training yearly. Prior studies commissioned by the DOC have recommended such training. The department has repeatedly failed to implement even such minimal requirements.

Massachusetts Prison Suicides

Last year [2006] alone, seven inmates killed themselves [in Massachusetts prisons]; and another's attempt left him brain dead; four have taken their lives so far this year [as of December 2007].

Department of Correction officials say the suicides are random and unrelated. But a [*Boston*] *Globe* Spotlight Team investigation of the deaths and detailed reconstruction of how they occurred found that they were far from random.

Most of the suicides came after careless errors and dangerous decisions by correction officials and the staff at UMass Correctional Health. And the trail of violence is far wider than the number of dead would indicate, as hundreds more inmates each year have wounded themselves or attempted suicide.

In fact, such incidents are soaring.

So common has it been to find a man with a makeshift noose around his neck that some correction officers have taken to carrying their own pocket tools to cut them down. The tally of suicide attempts and self-inflicted injuries—513 last year and more than 3,200 over the past decade—tells a story of deepening mental illness and misery behind the walls of the state's prisons, despite repeated calls for better training of officers and safer cells for mentally troubled inmates.

Beth Healy, Boston Globe, *December 9, 2007.*

Many prisoners deride the concept of special mental health treatment units as 'same guards, same treatment, different location'. They understand that the prison culture affects mental health clinicians as deeply as DOC employees. Indeed many 'lifers' [those prisoners with life sentences] and older prisoners speak eloquently about being subjected to behavior modification programs, aversive conditioning, electro-shock 'therapy,' forced administration of powerful sedatives and four-point restraints.

Nevertheless, against this reformist backdrop the DOC has seized the liberal momentum. In February [2008], four Custom Therapeutic Modules [CTMS] were delivered to MCI [Massachusetts Correctional Institute]-Cedar Junction. The CTMs are steel cages, measuring approximately 4' by 4' by 8', which contain a small opening for shackled legs and a metal stool. A sales slip shows that the DOC Central Office in Milford ordered the units at a cost of $15,000 each.

Can a person be 'cured' in a cage? Can humanization occur in a dehumanizing atmosphere? If prisoners need treatment, it is, in large part, for injuries from the institutional violence to which they are subjected in prison and within a society that wages war against its young, the poor and people of color.

The push for RTUs inverts cause and effect of disablement in the prison system. Any legislation, lawsuit or advocacy work which requires that abused and disabled prisoners be 'helped' to heal by the very entity which tortures them is no help at all. It is betrayal and collusion with state-sanctioned violence.

Periodical Bibliography

The following articles have been selected to supplement the diverse views presented in this chapter.

Marlene Busko	"Revolving-Prison-Door Phenomenon Seen in Mentally Ill Inmates," *Medscape Today*, January 16, 2009. www.medscape.com.
Marian Wright Edelman	"Juveniles Don't Belong in Adult Prisons," *Huffington Post*, August 4, 2008. www.huffingtonpost.com.
Marilyn Elias	"Is Adult Prison Best for Juveniles?" *USA Today*, September 20, 2006.
Sarah Kershaw	"New Rules for Confining the Mentally Ill," *New York Times*, April 25, 2007.
Ellen S. Podgor	"Throwing Away the Key," *Yale Law Journal*, February 21, 2007.
Michael Rothfeld	"Juvenile Prison System Needs Reform, Lawyers Say," *Los Angeles Times*, February 18, 2008.
Andrew Russ Sorkin	"How Long to Jail White-Collar Criminals?" *New York Times*, September 16, 2005.
M.J. Stephey	"De-criminalizing Mental Illness," *Time*, August 8, 2007.
Nicole Summer	"Powerless in Prison: Sexual Abuse Against Incarcerated Women," RH Reality Check, December 11, 2007. www.rhrealitycheck.org.
Rev Young	"A New Movement in Colorado," *A Voice for Juvenile Prison Reform*, September 21, 2009. http://avoiceforjuvenileprisonreform.kingscrossingfoundation.com.

For Further Discussion

Chapter 1

1. Joel Waldfogel cites evidence that shows that the threat of prison is not a deterrent for young offenders. Is Waldfogel talking about general deterrence or specific deterrence as defined by Bruce Bayley? How do you know?
2. Dana Pico argues that violent offenders should not be released just because they complete drug treatment programs. According to the *Shreveport Times*, if treatment programs were denied to violent offenders, would there still be a place for such programs in prison? Explain your reasoning.

Chapter 2

1. Thomas Sowell (in Chapter 1) argues that it is politically expedient for politicians to build fewer prisons because that frees money for giveaway programs. Glenn Loury suggests that law-and-order rhetoric is popular in part because of a subtext of racial fears. Whom do you believe is more persuasive on this issue? Why? Do you think politicians generally find it easier to be pro- or anti-prison? Why?
2. Robert Hooker and Robert Hirsh argue that "there is no direct relationship between incarceration rates and crime rates." What evidence does Heather Mac Donald provide to try to dispute this claim?
3. Does Theodore Dalrymple advocate the imprisonment of drug users simply for using? Why or why not? Does Michael Huemer suggest that drug users who commit other crimes should be allowed to go free? Explain why you think so or do not think so. Do you think Dalrymple

and Huemer could come to an agreement about who should and who should not be imprisoned? How?

Chapter 3

1. Harley G. Lappin states that America's prisons are humane. Craig Haney argues that certain prison conditions such as overcrowding are inhumane. Which author do you agree with? Why?
2. Why does Debra Saunders refer to J. Clark Kelso as "His Receivership"? Why does J. Clark Kelso begin his essay by praising Californians and identifying himself as one of them ("we must turn to our basic sense of what is right")?

Chapter 4

1. Carol Lloyd argues that having infants in prison with their mothers, as discussed by Suzanne Smalley, is a bad solution for children. Do you agree? Why or why not? Can you think of any better ways to address the problems that arise when mothers with young children are imprisoned? Explain.
2. Campaign for Youth Justice argues that the adult prison system is not a safe place for juveniles. Do you think that Susan Mortimer would agree that only juveniles should be kept out of adult prisons? Explain your reasoning.

Organizations to Contact

American Civil Liberties Union (ACLU)
125 Broad Street, 18th Floor, New York, NY 10004-2400
(888) 567-ACLU
e-mail: aclu@aclu.org
Web site: www.aclu.org

Founded in 1920, the ACLU is a national organization that works to defend civil liberties in the United States. It publishes various materials on the Bill of Rights, including on prisoners' rights, as well as regular in-depth reports, the newsletter *Civil Liberties*, and a set of handbooks on individual rights.

Amnesty International (AI)
322 Eighth Ave., New York, NY 10001
(212) 807-8400 • fax: (212) 463-9193
e-mail: admin-us@aiusa.org
Web site: www.amnesty.org

Made up of over 1.8 million members in over 150 countries, AI is dedicated to promoting human rights worldwide. Since its inception in 1961, the organization has focused much of its effort on the eradication of torture. AI maintains an active news Web site, distributes a large annual report on the state of human rights in every country (as well as numerous special reports on specific human rights issues), and publishes the monthly magazine the *Wire*.

The Brookings Institution
1775 Massachusetts Ave. NW, Washington, DC 20036
(202) 797-6000 • fax: (202) 797-6004
e-mail: communication@brookings.edu
Web site: www.brookings.edu

The institution, founded in 1927, is a think tank that conducts research and education in foreign policy, economics, government, and the social sciences. Its publications include the quarterly *Brookings Review* and periodic *Policy Briefs*.

Center for Alternative Sentencing and Employment Services (CASES)
346 Broadway, 8th Floor, New York, NY 10013
(212) 732-0076 • fax: (212) 571-0292
e-mail: info@cases.org
Web site: www.cases.org

CASES seeks to end what it views as the overuse of incarceration as a response to crime. It operates two alternative-sentencing programs in New York City: the Court Employment Project, which provides intensive supervision and services for felony offenders, and the Community Service Sentencing Project, which works with repeat misdemeanor offenders. The center advocates in court for such offenders' admission into its programs. CASES publishes various program brochures.

Corrections Connection
159 Burgin Parkway, Quincy, MA 02169
(617) 471-4445 • fax: (617) 770-3339
e-mail: editor@corrections.com
Web site: www.corrections.com

The Corrections Connection is committed to improving national and international correctional policy and to promoting the professional development of those working in the field of corrections. It offers a variety of books and correspondence courses on corrections and criminal justice.

Families Against Mandatory Minimums (FAMM)
1612 K Street NW, Suite 700, Washington, DC 20006
(202) 822-6700 • fax: (202) 822-6704
e-mail: famm@famm.org
Web site: www.famm.org

FAMM is an educational organization that works to repeal mandatory minimum sentences in the United States. It provides legislators, the public, and the media with information on and analyses of minimum-sentencing laws. FAMM publishes the quarterly newsletter *FAMM-gram*.

Human Rights Watch (HRW)
350 Fifth Ave., 34th Floor, New York, NY 10118-3299
(212) 290-4700 • fax: (212) 736-1300
e-mail: hrwnyc@hrw.org
Web site: www.hrw.org

In 1988, several large regional organizations dedicated to promoting human rights merged to form HRW, a global watchdog group. HRW publishes numerous books, policy papers, and special reports (including a comprehensive annual report), sponsors an annual film festival on human rights issues, and files lawsuits on behalf of those whose rights are violated.

National Center for Policy Analysis (NCPA)
12770 Coit Road, Suite 800, Dallas, TX 75251-1339
(972) 386-6272 • fax: (972) 386-0924
e-mail: publications@ncpa.org
Web site: www.ncpa.org

NCPA is a nonprofit public policy research institute that addresses a range of issues. In dealing with crime, it advocates more stringent prison sentences, the abolishment of parole, and restitution for crimes. Publications include the policy reports "Does Punishment Deter?" and "Crime and Punishment in Texas."

National Center on Institutions and Alternatives (NCIA)
7222 Ambassador Road, Baltimore, MD 21244
(410) 265-1490
Web site: www.ncianet.org

NCIA is a criminal justice foundation that encourages community-based alternatives to prison that it believes are more effective in providing education, training, and the personal skills required for the rehabilitation of nonviolent offenders. The center advocates doubling "good conduct" credit for the early release of nonviolent first-time offenders in the federal system to make room for violent offenders. NCIA publishes books, reports, and the periodic newsletters the *Sentencing Advocate* and *Jail Suicide/Mental Health Update.*

National Crime Prevention Council (NCPC)
2345 Crystal Drive, Suite 500, Arlington, VA 22202
(202) 466-6272 • fax: (202) 296-1356
Web site: www.ncpc.org

The NCPC provides training and technical assistance to groups and individuals interested in crime prevention. It advocates job training and recreation programs as a means to reduce crime and violence. The council, which sponsors the Take a Bite Out of Crime campaign, publishes the newsletter *Catalyst*, which is published ten times a year.

National Criminal Justice Reference Service (NCJRS)
U.S. Department of Justice, Rockville, MD 20849-6000
(800) 851-3420
Web site: www.ncjrs.org

The National Criminal Justice Reference Service is one of the most extensive sources of information on criminal justice in the world. Its Web site provides topical searches and reading lists on many areas of criminal justice. Numerous publications on the justice system, drugs, crime, and other topics are available through its Web site.

National Prison Project
915 Fifteenth Street NW, 7th Floor, Washington, DC 20005
(202) 393-4930
e-mail: mtartaglia@npp-aclu.org
Web site: www.aclu.org/prison

Formed in 1972 by the American Civil Liberties Union, the project serves as a national resource center and litigates cases to strengthen and protect adult and juvenile offenders' Eighth

Amendment rights. It opposes electronic monitoring of offenders and the privatization of prisons. The project publishes the quarterly *National Prison Project Journal* and booklets such as the *Prisoners' Assistance Directory*.

Prison Fellowship Ministries (PFM)
44180 Riverside Parkway, Lansdowne, VA 20176
(877) 478-0100
Web site: www.prisonfellowship.org

Prison Fellowship Ministries encourages Christians to work in prisons and to assist communities in ministering to prisoners, ex-offenders, and their families. It works toward establishing a fair and effective criminal justice system and trains volunteers for in-prison ministries. Its publications include the *Jubilee* newsletter and numerous books, including *Born Again* and *Life Sentence*.

The Sentencing Project
514 Tenth Street NW, Suite 1000, Washington, DC 20004
(202) 628-0871 • fax: (202) 628-1091
e-mail: staff@sentencingproject.org
Web site: www.sentencingproject.org

The project seeks to provide public defenders and other public officials with information on establishing and improving alternative sentencing programs that provide convicted persons with positive and constructive options to incarceration. It promotes increased public understanding of the sentencing process and alternative sentencing programs. It publishes reports such as "No Exit: The Expanding Use of Life Sentences in America," and "Federal Crack Cocaine Sentencing."

U.S. Department of Justice, Federal Bureau of Prisons
320 First Street NW, Washington, DC 20534
e-mail: info@bop.gov
Web site: www.bop.gov

The Federal Bureau of Prisons works to protect society by confining offenders in the controlled environments of prison and community-based facilities. It believes in providing work and other self-improvement opportunities within these facilities to assist offenders in becoming law-abiding citizens. The bureau publishes the annual book *The State of the Bureau.*

Bibliography of Books

Curtis R. Blakeley	*America's Prisons: The Movement Towards Profit and Privatization*. Boca Raton, FL: Brown Walker, 2005.
Demico Booth	*Why Are So Many Black Men in Prison? A Comprehensive Account of How and Why the Prison Industry Has Become a Predatory Entity in the Lives of African-American Men*. 2nd ed. Memphis, TN: Full Surface, 2007.
James H. Bruton	*The Big House: Life Inside a Supermax Security Prison*. Osceola, WI: Voyageur, 2004.
Anne-Marie Cusac	*Cruel and Unusual: The Culture of Punishment in America*. New Haven, CT: Yale University Press, 2009.
Theodore Dalrymple	*Romancing Opiates: Pharmacological Lies and the Addiction Bureaucracy*. Rev. ed. New York: Encounter Books, 2006.
Laura B. Edge	*Locked Up: A History of the U.S. Prison System*. Minneapolis, MN: Twenty-First Century Books, 2009.
Alec C. Ewald and Brandon Rottinghaus, eds.	*Criminal Disenfranchisement in an International Perspective*. New York: Cambridge University Press, 2009.
Renny Golden	*War on the Family: Mothers in Prison and the Families They Leave Behind*. New York: Taylor & Francis, 2005.

Victor Hassine *Life Without Parole: Living in Prison Today*. 4th ed. New York: Oxford University Press, 2008.

Michael Jacobson *Downsizing Prisons: How to Reduce Crime and End Mass Incarceration*. New York: New York University, 2005.

Paula Johnson, Joyce A. Logan, and Angela J. Davis *Inner Lives: Voices of African American Women in Prison*. New York: New York University Press, 2003.

Heather Mac Donald *Are Cops Racist?* Chicago: Ivan R. Dee, 2003.

Bill Masters, ed. *The New Prohibition: Voices of Dissent Challenge the Drug War*. St. Paul, MN: Accurate, 2004.

Christian Parenti *Lockdown America*. Brooklyn: Verso, 2000.

Katherine Irene Pettus *Felony Disenfranchisement in America: Historical Origins, Institutional Racism, and Modern Consequences*. El Paso, TX: LFB, 2004.

Mary Beth Pfeiffer *Crazy in America: The Hidden Tragedy of Our Criminalized Mentally Ill*. New York: Carroll & Graf, 2007.

Travis C. Pratt *Addicted to Incarceration: Corrections Policy and the Politics of Misinformation in the United States*. Thousand Oaks, CA: Sage, 2008

Lorna A. Rhodes	*Total Confinement: Madness and Reason in the Maximum Security Prison.* Berkeley and Los Angeles: University of California Press, 2004.
Donna Selman	*Punishment for Sale: Private Prisons and Big Business.* Lanham, MD: Rowman & Littlefield, 2009.
Sharon Shalev	*Supermax: Controlling Risk Through Solitary Confinement.* Devon, UK: Willan, 2009.
Silja J.A. Talvi	*Women Behind Bars: The Crisis of Women in the Prison System.* Berkeley, CA: Seal, 2007.
E. Fuller Torrey	*The Insanity Offense: How America's Failure to Treat the Seriously Mentally Ill Endangers Its Citizens.* New York: Norton, 2008.
Bert Useem and Anne Morrison Piehl	*Prison State: The Challenge of Mass Incarceration.* New York: Cambridge University Press, 2008.
Bruce Western	*Punishment and Inequality in America.* New York: Russell Sage Foundation, 2007.
James Q. Wilson and Richard J. Herrnstein	*Crime & Human Nature: The Definitive Study of the Causes of Crime.* New York: Free Press, 1985.
James Q. Wilson and Joan Petersilia, eds.	*Crime: Public Policies for Crime Control.* Richmond, CA: ICS Press, 2002.

Franklin Zimring and Gordon Hawkins	*Incapacitation: Penal Confinement and the Restraint of Crime.* New York: Oxford University Press, 1997.

Index

A

ABC News, 124
Administrative Remedy Program, 129–130
Adrenaline, 147
African Americans
  drug crimes, 75–76
  education, 58
  lenient punishment, 74
  prison population, 58–60, 62–65, 72
  violent crime, 72–73
Age of Pericles, 116
Alcohol, 93–94, 96, 101
Allegheny County Mental Health Court (MHC), 190
Allen, Charlotte, 74
Allen County Jail (Indiana), 140–144
Alternative sentencing, 40–47
American Bar Association's Task Force on Effective Criminal Sanctions, 41, 45
Amherst College, 117, 118
Amnesty International, 149–150
Amphetamines, 89
Annals of Emergency Medicine (journal), 148
Anti–Drug Abuse Act, 76
Anti-incarceration activists, 181, 182
Apologies, 46
Arizona, 92–97, 179
Arsenault, Walter, 79
Assault, 16
Associated Content (Web site), 163
Associate Warden, 127
Avergun, Jodi L., 86–91
Aversive conditioning, 198

B

Bahamas, 59
Balser, Ruth, 195
Beccaria, Cesare, 26
Becka, Holly, 16
Behavior modification, 198
Belarus, 59, 182
Bias, Len, 77
Billboard Project, 46–47
Bipolar disease, 187–188
BlackLetter Law Journal, 114
Blackmun, Harry, 116
Bolivia, 173
Boone, David, 32–33
Boston Globe (newspaper), 194, 195, 197
Bozeman, William P., 148
Braz, Rose, 46
Breathalyzers, 41, 45
British Forensic Science Service, 146, 148
Brown, Gerald, 101
Brown, Jerry, 157, 158, 160
Brown University, 57
Browne, Jeffrey, 95
Burger, Warren, 116
Burrell, Roy, 31, 34
Business Week (magazine), 164
Butterfield, Fox, 49

C

Caddo Correctional Center, 31–33
Cahill, Clyde, 77
California
  alternative sentencing, 43
  chemical castration in, 46
  early release program, 159
  educational programs in prison facilities, 179
  ignition interlock breathalyzers, 45
  Jim Crow laws, 114
  leniency for African Americans, 74
  maximum security prisons, 138
  mentally ill prisoners, 192
  prison costs, 18, 151–155
  prison overcrowding, 154
  prison population, 132
California Department of Corrections and Rehabilitation, 157
California Prison Health Care System, 151, 156–160
Cambodia, 173
Campaign for Youth Justice (CFYJ), 174–179
Canada, 59
Capital punishment, 123, 181
Carlson, Joseph, 166
Cash, Johnny, 41
Cassidy, Charles, 38
Cate, Matt, 158
CBS News, 119
CeaseFire Outreach, 42
Cellucci, Paul, 119
Center for Law and Justice, 115
Centers for Disease Control and Prevention Task Force on Community Preventive Services, 176
Chaotic thinking, 189
Checkley, Dorn, 56
Chemical castration, 46
Chen, Stephanie, 14
Chicago Tribune (newspaper), 171
Children. *See* Juveniles and children
Chin, Denny, 164
China, 58
City Journal, 71
Clarke, Conor, 117–120
Clarke, Harold, 196
Clinton, Bill, 83
Clinton, Hillary, 72
Cocaine and crack, 76–81, 167
Coke County Juvenile Justice Center, 16
Colorado, 19
Colorado Springs Gazette (newspaper), 15
Columbia University, 26, 28, 81
Commission on Safety and Abuse in America's Prisons, 135
Community service, 43
Community Services Society, 115
Community supervision, 50
Conducted-energy devices (CEDs), 143
  See also Stun technology
Connecticut, 44, 49, 114
Convention Against Torture, 184
Convention on the Rights of the Child (CRC), 184
Coolican, Joseph, 36
Corporate criminals, 41, 45
Correctional workers
  communication with inmates, 126
  mental health training, 191–192

misconduct, 130
role, 126
stun technology, 142, 146
violence against prisoners, 195
weapons, 140–144

Corrections Compendium (journal), 166
Corrections Corporation of America (CCA), 14–15
Costs. *See* Prison costs
Council of State Governments Justice Center, 190
Crack cocaine, 76–81
Crime
drug addiction and, 102
effects of prison, 81–82
nonviolent offenders, 31, 44, 163–164
prison as deterrence, 20–24
victimless crimes, 55
violent crime, 16
white-collar crime, 163–164
See also Drug offenders; Violent crime
Crime rates, 22, 25
Crime reduction, 49–50
Crist, Charlie, 119
Critical Resistance, 46
Cruel and unusual punishment, 152, 181
Cuba, 182
Cusac, Anne-Marie, 145–150
Cutting Corrections: Earned Time Policies for State Prisoners (National Conference of States Legislatures), 18

D

"D-Boys" gang, 143
Dallas Morning News (newspaper), 16
Dalrymple, Theodore, 98–103
Daniels, Anthony, 98
David, Ruth, 40–47
Davis, Stephanie, 55
De Tocqueville, Alexis, 119
DEA (Drug Enforcement Administration), 79, 86, 87
Death penalty, 123, 181
Death Penalty Information Center (DPIC), 123
Death row, 123–124
Deaths from stun technology, 144, 146–148
Decriminalize Prostitution Now Coalition, 55
Defending America's Most Vulnerable: Safe Access to Drug Treatment and Child Protection Act of 2004, 88
Degradation, 194–196
Deitch, Michele, 16
Delaware, 49
Delusions, 189
Democracy Now! Online, 115
Dental care, 152, 153, 159, 178
Denver Post (newspaper), 19
Depo-Provera, 46
Depression, 187–188
Deterrence
general deterrence, 21, 23–24
prison as, 20–29
research, 26–28
specific deterrence, 21–23
stun technology, 144
white-collar crime, 163

Dickens, Charles, 99
DiMascio, William, 36–39
Disability Law Center, 194, 195
Dropouts, 59
Drug Enforcement Administration (DEA), 79, 86, 87
Drug offenders
- African Americans, 75–76
- alternatives to prison, 44
- crack cocaine, 76–81
- crime offenses and, 102
- DUI (driving under the influence), 93–94, 96
- effect in poor neighborhoods, 102–103
- heroin, 99–100
- justness of imprisonment, 98–103
- mandatory minimum sentencing, 86–91, 94, 168
- marijuana, 95
- methamphetamines, 88–89
- one-strike rule, 83–84
- positive effect of prison, 99–100
- pregnant women, 109
- prison population, 80–81, 154
- prosecution of drug traffickers, 89–91
- PROTECT Act and, 87–89
- right to use drugs, 106–109
- treatment ineffectiveness, 101
- United Kingdom (UK), 98–103
- unjustness of imprisonment, 104–111
- War on Drugs, 110–111
- women, 167

See also Substance abuse
Drug Policy Commission (UK), 99
Drug prohibition, 106
Drug Treatment Alternatives to Prison program, 43, 44
"Dry stuns", 141
Duffy, Michael, 32, 34
DUI (driving under influence), 93–94, 96

E

Eckley, Ephraim R., 116
Economist (magazine), 55
Education
- Arizona prison facilities, 179
- California prison facilities, 179
- college courses in prisons, 118–120
- education programs and time off, 18–19
- high-school dropouts, 59
- juvenile offenders, 176, 178–179
- marginalization and, 58
- poverty, 68
- prison costs and education spending, 18–19, 49, 50
- recidivism and, 19

Eighth Amendment, 152, 181, 182, 184
Electro-muscular-disruption technology, 143
  See also Stun technology
Electro-shock therapy, 198
Electronic Defense Technology (EDT), 146, 149
Electronic monitoring devices, 50, 51
Electronic riot shields, 146
Elsner, Alan, 123, 124
Employment of ex-convicts, 82–84
Enron, 163–164
Escape from prison, 16, 51

F

Fagan, Jeffrey, 81–83
Faith-based rehabilitation programs, 44
Federal Bureau of Investigation (FBI), 43, 130
Federal Bureau of Prisons, 44, 125–127, 130
Feeley, Malcolm, 137, 138
Fellner, Jamie, 186
Fines, 41
Finland, 173
Fitzgerald, Larry, 124
Florida
  chemical castration, 46
  costs of incarceration, 18
  crime and sentencing research, 25, 28
  death penalty, 123
  voting rights of convicts, 119
Florida Department of Corrections, 18
Folsom Prison Blues (Cash), 41
Food in prisons, 123–124
Forbes (magazine), 40
Fourteenth Amendment, 114–116
France, 59, 173
Franklin, Stanford, 108
Fraser, David, 50, 51
Fries, Ken, 142, 144
Frontline (TV show), 79
Fulford, Clyde, 84

G

Gangs, 143
Garland, David, 61
Gathright, Alan, 15
GED (general education development degree), 38, 179
General deterrence, 21, 23–24
Genest, Mike, 160
Georgia, 46, 74
Germany, 173
Ghana, 173
Giddings, Daniel, 36–39
Gilroy, Leonard, 15
Gleckman, Howard, 164
Goodson, Mark, 147
Grace, Robert, 84–85
Grant, Louise, 15
Greece, 114, 116
Grossman, Andrew M., 180–185
Gumbel, Bryant, 119

H

Hallucinations, 189, 191
Hamlin, Lynn B., 36–38
Hampshire County Correctional Facility (Massachusetts), 117–120
Haney, Craig, 131–138
Hart, Charles, 140
Hayden, Joseph "Jazz", 113, 115, 116
Hayden v. Pataki (2006), 113, 115
Health care for prisoners
  California program, 151, 156–160
  correctional officer misconduct and, 195
  costs, 158
  dental care, 152, 153, 158, 159
  drug users, 154
  juvenile offenders, 178
  kidney transplants, 124
  mental health, 152, 159
  prison overcrowding, 133–134, 154–155
Healy, Beth, 195–197

Heart problems and stun technology, 143, 146–147
Henderson, Thelton E., 157–158
Henry, Stuart, 27
Heritage Foundation, 180
Heroin, 99–100
High-school dropouts, 59
Hirsh, Robert, 92–97
Hispanic persons, 58, 73
HIV, 177
Homicide/murder, 41, 45, 72–73, 79–80
Hooker, Robert, 92–97
Hoover Institution, 48
Huemer, Michael, 104–111
Hungary, 173
Husak, Douglas, 106
Hynes, Charles, 43, 44

I

Iceland, 173
Idleness of prisoners, 16, 136
Ignition interlock breathalyzers, 45
In My Shoes program, 41
In Your State: Prison Costs (PBS broadcast), 18
Incarceration Nation conference, 27
India, 40
Indiana Women's Prison, 166, 168
Individuals with Disabilities Education Act (IDEA), 179
InnerChange Freedom Initiative, 44
Inside-Out (education program), 118
International Centre for Prison Studies, 58
International Covenant on Civil and Political Rights, 184
International treaties, 184–185
Iowa, 89
Ireland, 114, 173

J

Jail, 33
Japan, 59
Jarosz, Francesca, 168
Jim Crow laws, 114, 116
John Jay College of Criminal Justice, 168
Johnson, Ben, 112–116
Juan, Stephen, 148
Juvenile Justice and Delinquency Prevention Act (JJDPA), 177
Juveniles and children
- adult prisons and, 174–179
- educational services for juvenile offenders, 176, 178–179
- health care, 178
- incarceration rates, 175
- life without parole, 180–185
- mental disorders, 175–176
- murders per capita, 182
- prison nurseries, 165–173
- prison rape, 175, 177
- PROTECT Act, 87–89
- recidivism, 176–177
- solitary confinement, 175
- suicide, 175–176

K

Kansas, 168
Kaufman, Dennis, 149
Kazakhstan, 182
Keenan, John, 43
Kelso, J. Clark, 151–158, 160

Kennedy, Matthew, 83–84
Kennedy, Randall, 78
Kidney transplant, 124
King, Martin Luther, 72
Konopnicki, Bill, 95

L

LaFleur, Jennifer, 16
Lambrix, Mike, 123
Landis, Harry, 146–147
Langan, Patrick, 75
Lappin, Harley G., 125–130
Lauritsen, Janet, 74
Law & Order (TV show), 26, 29
Law enforcement, 73
Lawrence, Alison, 18
Learning disabilities, 179
LeBlanc, Jimmy, 34
Lee, David S., 28–29
Lethal force, 138
Levitt, Steven, 22
Lewis, John, 38
Libby, Scooter, 73
Life without parole, 180–185
Lloyd, Carol, 170–173
Locke, John, 119
Los Angeles Times (newspaper), 22
Louisiana, 31–33, 93
Loury, Glenn, 57–70

M

Mac Donald, Heather, 71–85
MacArthur Foundation Research Network on Adolescent Development and Juvenile Justice, 176
Madison Street Maricopa County Jail, 179
Madoff, Bernie, 164
Maine, 116
Malta, 173
Mandatory minimum sentencing, 37–38, 86–91, 94–97, 168
Manhattan Institute, 71
Marable, Manning, 119
Marginalization, 58, 68–70
Marijuana, 95
Marqui, Joshua, 124
Maryland, 45, 114
Massachusetts, 117–120, 193–198
Massachusetts Correctional Institute-Cedar Junction, 198
Massachusetts Correctional Legal Services, 194, 195
Maximum security prisons, 138
Maykuth, Andrew, 39
McCrary, Justin, 28–29
McDermit, John, 147
McDonald, Patrick, 36–37, 39
Medi-Cal, 153
Mental health
  ability to follow instructions and, 186
  correctional officer training, 191–192
  juveniles, 175–176, 178
  medication, 187, 188
  mental health services in prisons, 152, 159, 188–189
  prison conditions and, 193–198
  prison overcrowding and, 133, 135
  prisoners with mental disorders, 186–192
See also Suicides in prisons
Methamphetamines, 88–89, 168
Mexico, 84, 172
Michigan, 49

Miller, William R., 101
Minnesota, 46, 114
Mississippi, 93
Missouri, 44, 89, 95
Model prisons, 32–33
Morgan, John, 143
Mortimer, Susan, 193–198
Moskos, Peter, 108
Murder/homicide, 41, 45, 72–73, 79–80
Music City Syndicate, 55

N

NAACP (National Association for the Advancement of Colored People), 115
Napolitano, Janet, 93
National Catholic Reporter (newspaper), 177
National Center for Correctional Healthcare Studies, 149
National Conference of State Legislatures, 18
Nebraska, 46–47, 168
New Mexico, 44
New York
- drug programs, 43
- effect of prison and crime rates, 82
- order maintenance in Riker's Island jail, 138
- prison nurseries, 168
- prison rape, 177
- prison versus education expenditures, 18
- voting rights for convicts, 113

New York Times (newspaper), 49, 51, 77, 78, 118
New Zealand, 50, 173
Newsweek (magazine), 165
Nonviolent offenders. *See specific nonviolent crimes*
Nova Products, Inc., 147

O

Obama, Barack, 72, 84, 113
Observer (UK newspaper), 99, 102
Oceano, Jack, 163
O'Donnell, Jayne, 163
Office of Inspector General, 130
Office of National Drug Control Policy (ONDCP), 105, 106
Ohio, 114, 116
Oklahoma, 18
"One-strike" rule for public housing, 83–84
Online NewsHour, 95
Oregon, 46, 49, 114, 124
Organ transplants, 124
Ott, Dwight, 39
Overcrowding. *See* Prison overcrowding
Owens, Major, 78

P

Pakistan, 173
Panama, 182
Paraguay, 182
Pardons, 116
Parish, Anthony A., 143
Parole, 19, 159, 195
Pataki, Hayden v. (2006), 113, 115
Pay for Your Prison Stay Programs, 44
PBS (Public Broadcasting Service), 18, 79
Pennsylvania, 18

Pennsylvania Prison Society, 36, 38
Pericles, 116
Personal responsibility, 105
Philadelphia Inquirer (newspaper), 36–37
Philippines, 182
Pico, Dana, 35–39
Pittsburgh Coalition Against Pornography, 56
Plea bargaining, 95–96
Police murder, 36–37
Pornography, 56
Poverty, 59, 63, 68, 102–103
Prator, Steve, 31
Pregnant women, 109
Prison camps, 163
Prison costs
  Arizona, 93
  California, 18, 151–155, 158
  education spending versus, 18–19, 49, 50
  Florida, 18
  food and clothing, 18
  health care, 158
  Louisiana, 34
  New York, 18
  Oklahoma, 18
  Pennsylvania, 18
  private companies, 14
  security, 18
  societal benefits versus, 60
  Texas, 18
  Wisconsin, 18
Prison Fellowship, 44
Prison inmates
  demographics, 62, 72
  drug offenders, 80–81, 94, 98–103
  economics and, 14
  growth rate, 132, 134
  imprisonment rates 2000–2007, 62
  national average, 33
  organizational stability and, 132–133
  prison nurseries, 165–173
  prison rape, 177
  race, 59, 63–65, 71–85
  riots and, 15
  United States, 43, 58–60
  violent crime and, 80
  See also Women
Prison overcrowding
  costs, 95
  danger, 15, 134–136
  early release, 154, 159
  health issues, 133–134
  inhumanity, 131–138
  mental health and, 187
  psychological effect, 133, 135
  white-collar crime and, 163
Prison oversight, 125–130
Prison without parole, 37–38
Private companies managing prisons, 14–16
Probation, 41, 43
Project for Violence Prevention, 44–45
Property offenses, 81
Prostitution, 55
PROTECT Act, 87–89
Psychotropic medication, 187
Public Broadcasting Service (PBS), 18, 79
Public housing, 83–84
Public shaming, 41, 46–47

Q

Quaker United Nations Office, 172
Quakers, 195

R

Race. *See* African Americans; Hispanic persons
Race, Crime, and the Law (Kennedy), 78
Race industry, 72
Ramirez, Richardson v. (1974), 116
RAND Corporation, 190
Rangel, Charles, 78
Rapadas, Leonardo M., 90
Rape, 41, 175, 177
Rayl, Ron, 142
REACT (Remote Electronically Activated Control Technology), 146
Recidivism
  education and, 19
  juveniles, 176–177
  percentage, 43
  prison nurseries and, 168–169
  rates, 94
Reducing Demand for Prostitution (National Institute for Justice), 55
Rehabilitation
  Arizona, 93–94
  drug offenders, 101
  faith-based rehabilitation programs, 44
  funding, 93
  "Great Lies", 21
  inneffectiveness, 35–39
  prison overcrowding and, 15
  specific deterrence, 24
  substance abuse and, 30–34
Rehnquist, William, 116
Reiman, Jeffrey, 114
Religion, 44
Research
  crime deterrence and prison, 26–28
  education programs and time off, 18–19
  juveniles in adult prisons, 176–177
  mentally ill prisoners, 188
  recidivism, 43
Restorative Justice program, 46
Retribution, 61
Reyes-Camarena, Horacio Alberto, 124
Rhode Island, 114
The Rich Get Richer and the Poor Get Prison (Reiman), 114
Richardson v. Ramirez (1974), 116
Ridgely, M. Susan, 190
Right to use drugs, 106–108
Rikers Island, 138
Riots, 15
Riveland, Chase, 149
Robbery, 41
Roberts, John, 116
Robinson, Bryan, 124
Rocky Mountain News (newspaper), 15
Roosevelt University in Chicago, 145
Roper v. Simmons (2005), 181, 183–184
Russia, 58, 59

S

Sabol, William J., 172
Saltzburg, Stephen, 41, 45
Sampson, Robert, 74
San Quentin prison, 158
Sanchez-Craig, Martha, 101

Saunders, Debra, 156–160
Schall, Jason, 114
Schizophrenia, 187, 189
Schriro, Dora, 95
Schulze, Robert, 16
Schwarzenegger, Arnold, 157, 158, 159
Segal, Geoffrey, 14–15
Self-inflicted injury, 189, 192, 197
Sensenbrenner, Jim, 88
Sentencing
- alternative sentencing, 40–47
- guidelines, 43
- life without parole, 180–185
- mandatory minimums, 37–38, 86–91, 94–97, 168
- plea bargaining, 95–96
- prison without parole, 37–38

Shaming, 41, 46–47
Shoplifting, 169
Shreveport Times (newspaper), 30–34
Sillen, Robert, 158
Simmons, Roper v. (2005), 181, 183–184
Simon, Jonathan, 137, 138
Slutkin, Gary, 44–45
Smalley, Suzanne, 165–169
Social responsibility, 66–68
Soering, Jens, 177
Sokoloff, Natalie, 168
Solitary confinement
- death row, 123–124
- disciplinary segregation, 127, 138
- juveniles, 175
- mental health and, 187, 194

Sotomayor, Sonia, 112, 113, 116
Sowell, Thomas, 48–52
Spain, 173
Special education services, 179
Special Housing Units, 127
Specific deterrence, 21–23
Spotlight Team of *Boston Globe*, 196, 197
Stanford University, 48
Start, Armond, 149
Stimson, Charles D., 180–185
Stone, Steve, 141
"Strawberries", 78
Stun Tech (company), 145, 146, 149
Stun technology
- conducted-energy devices (CEDs), 143
- dangers, 145–150
- deaths, 144, 146–148
- deterrence, 144
- "dry stuns", 141
- electro-muscular-disruption technology, 143
- heart problems, 143, 146–147
- lawsuits, 142
- physical effects, 143
- prisoner violence, 140–141
- stun guns, 137
- Tasers, 139–144

Stutman, Robert, 79
Substance abuse
- crime commission, 31
- DUI arrests, 93–94
- rehabilitation and, 30–34
- treatment programs, 44

See also Drug offenders
Suicides in prisons
- isolation factor, 175–176
- Massachusetts, 194
- mental illness, 189, 196–197
- prevention, 141
- prisoner abuse, 16
- statistics 1990–2004, 128

The Super (movie), 45
"Supermax" prisons, 138
Surveillance, 137
Swern, Anne, 43

T

Taser International, 141
Testosterone, 46
Texas
  chemical castration, 46
  death row, 123
  incarceration rates, 93
  prison costs, 18
  prison nurseries, 168
  prison population, 132
  stun technology, 146
  turnover rate of prison employees, 15–16
Texas Coalition to Abolish the Death Penalty, 123
Texas Department of Corrections, 124
Texas Department of Criminal Justice, 44, 147
Texas Senate Criminal Justice Committee, 15–16
Tolstoy, Leo, 67
Tomlin, Angela, 167
Toomer, Devan, 169
Toomer, Devion, 169
Torture, 182
Tse, Tomoeh Murakami, 164

U

Unemployment, 59
United Kingdom (UK), 49, 50–52, 99, 173
United Nations, 173
United Nations Committee Against Torture, 150
University of California, Santa Cruz, 131
University of Colorado, 104
University of Illinois, 45
University of Michigan, 26, 28
University of Nebraska, 166
University of Pennsylvania, 25
University of the Pacific McGeorge Law School, 151
U.S. Bureau of Justice Statistics, 73, 75
U.S. Bureau of Prisons, 146, 149–150
U.S. Congress, 127
U.S. Constitution, 114, 116, 125, 152, 180–182, 185
U.S. Department of Corrections, 93, 176
U.S. Department of Justice Bureau of Justice Statistics (BJS), 175, 188
U.S. Government Accounting Office, 127, 136
U.S. House of Representatives, 78, 88
U.S. Justice Department, 41, 74, 87, 89–91, 127
U.S. Marshals Service, 146
U.S. Sentencing Commission, 77, 90
U.S. Supreme Court, 116, 181–183
USA Today (newspaper), 163, 164
Utter, Jessica, 167

V

Vehicle breathalyzers, 41, 45
Venezuela, 84

Vermont, 49, 116
Victimless crimes, 55
Violence Against Babies and Small Children Living in Prison With Their Mothers (Quaker United Nations Office), 172
Violent crime
  African Americans and, 72–73, 79–80
  definition, 41
  mental illness, 189
  prison statistics, 80
  rehabilitation, 36–37
  voting rights and, 113–114
Virginia, 114
Vision care, 178
Vocational training, 176, 179
Voting Rights Act, 114
Voting rights of convicts, 112–120

W

Waldfogel, Joel, 25–29
Waldon, Alton, 78
Walker, Leslie, 196
Wall Street Journal (newspaper), 14
War on Drugs, 110–111
Warden, 127, 129
Washington Post (newspaper), 108, 164
Washington State Department of Corrections, 149
Weber State Police Academy, 20
Weber State University, 20–24
Weekly Standard (periodical), 74
West, Heather C., 172
Western, Bruce, 59
Wharton School, 25
White-collar crime, 163–164
WholeHearted (anti-pornography program), 56
Wiehe, Jeff, 139–144
William Mead Homes (public housing), 84
Willing, Richard, 163
Wilson, James Q., 22
Wisconsin, 18, 167
Wisconsin Department of Corrections, 149
Women
  crack cocaine use, 78
  drug use and pregnant women, 109
  mothers and children in prison, 165–173
  prison population, 172
  prostitution, 55–56, 78
  stun technology and, 141, 142
Wood, Jimmy, 147
Work release, 33

Y

Yothers, Greg, 117–120